Family History in Schools

D. J. Steel and L. Taylor

PHILLIMORE

1973
Published by
PHILLIMORE & CO. LTD.
London and Chichester

Head Office: Shopwyke Hall,
Chichester, Sussex, England

[in collaboration with
Environmental History Ltd.
London Road, Wokingham, Berks.]

372.89,

ISBN 0 900592 60 5

Text set by Phillimore in 11pt. Baskerville
Printed in Great Britain by Eyre & Spottiswoode Ltd.,
Her Majesty's Printers, at Grosvenor Press, Portsmouth.

GRANNIE
1891-1970

Schoolgirl, 1906
(aged 15)

Bridesmaid, 1913
(aged 22)

At time of marriage, 1922
(aged 31)

ME
1963 -

Children Marry, 1962

Grannie and me, 1966

In my schooldays, history was concerned mainly with the lives of the famous or infamous and their effect on the fortunes and misfortunes of nations . . . The present-day student can, if he so wishes, study a topic which has been covered time and again by professional and student historians, but a Family History is a unique and personal study, and for this reason carries more weight and conviction.

Len Walker, Mature Student,
Berkshire College of Education (1971).

This series is dedicated to the memory
of the late W.E. Tate who did so much
to encourage interest in Environmental
History both in schools and among the
general public.

Contents

Illustrations

Preface

TO MOST PEOPLE, 'Family History' conjures up an image of wizened antiquarians in draughty vestries, blowing the dust off musty records written in indecipherable hands. We put forward for the consideration of the open-minded primary or secondary teacher, a new approach to history, in which the average child can be engaged upon a personal, original and genuine enquiry. In it he discovers for himself the main classes of evidence used by historians and uses them to study the last five or six generations of his own family. Whilst some attention is given in this volume to traditional genealogical sources, the emphasis has been laid upon oral evidence and upon those forms of documentary and archaeological evidence which are to be found in most homes.

In recent years 'The Family' has figured prominently in several Schools' Council projects. Family History has received rather less attention, but has not been without its advocates. Mentioned in a U.N.E.S.C.O. International seminar in 1951,[1] it began to make serious claims for consideration in the late 1960s. A short note in the I.A.A.M. publication *The Teaching of History in Secondary Schools* (1966),[2] was followed by a much longer one in Gosden and Sylvester's *History for the Average Child* (1968).[3] The approach has also found favour with George Ewart Evans, with whose work on oral history it has so much in common. His plea for Family History in schools, which appeared first in an article in the *Times Educational Supplement* in 1969,[4] was later developed in the concluding pages of *Where Beards Wag All* (1971).[5] Katherine Moore's *Family Fortunes: A Story of Social Change* (1969) used fictitious families to illustrate social change and, in a short appendix, suggested that children should use their own family histories in a similar way. The same general approach has been suggested by R. Wake, H.M. Staff Inspector for History[6] and Margaret West, Inspector of Schools for Wolverhampton.[7]

Nevertheless, few teachers seem to have developed Family History as an integral part of their work. A notable exception is Brendan Murphy, the Headmaster of St. Cuthbert's Primary School, Wigan, who has been operating a very successful scheme for a number of years.[8] At the Secondary level, a limited Family History project has been adovated by M.L. Andrews of Clee Humberstone Foundation School, Cleethorpes,[9] and extensive interviewing of old people has been undertaken by Secondary pupils in Sheffield.[10] Richard Fox of Kirkby Fields College of Education, Liverpool, has pioneered interesting work with students.

Many of the suggestions in this book derive from the experience of 18 teachers in six Primary and five Secondary Berkshire and Hampshire schools. Working with over 700 children, they have collaborated with us to test and modify the scheme originally outlined in our booklet *Family History in Schools: An Interdisciplinary Experiment* (1968). Their reports (see Chapters 13 and 14) suggest that Family History has been validated with children of varying ages and abilities sufficiently to warrant publication. Teaching Family History has its problems, as has every sort of teaching, but in the experience of those who have co-operated with us, the problems are much less serious than one might suppose, and in almost all cases solutions have been devised to enable children with special family difficulties to participate fully.

As well as its purely historical aims, Family History has important implications for interdisciplinary work and for the relationship of the school to parents and the community at large. History is about people and for the child we have found no better approach to the past than through the study of his own people, his family:

Don Steel
Lawrence Taylor

Berkshire College of Education

Notes and References

1. C.F. Hill, *Suggestions on the Teaching of History* (1953), p.49.

2. I.A.A.M., *The Teaching of History in Secondary Schools* (1966), p.33.

3. P.H.J.H. Gosden and D.W. Sylvester, *op. cit.*, pp.21-2.

4. 'History in the Family', *Times Educational Supplement*, 14 March 1969, p.851.

5. George Ewart Evans, *op. cit.*, p.281.

6. R. Wake, 'History as a Separate Discipline: The Case', in *Teaching History*, vol. 1, no. 3 (1970), p.154: 'Two unfailingly rewarding topics are: the day I was born; My great-grandfather/mother'.

7. Margaret West, 'History and the Younger Child', in *Teaching History*, vol. 1, no. 4 (1970), pp.259-262.

8. See Brendan Murphy, 'History in the Family I', in *Teaching History*, vol. 2, no. 5 (1971), pp.1-8.

9. M.L. Andrews, 'History for Life', in *Teaching History*, vol. 1, no. 3 (1970), p.210.

10. E. Fearn, 'Working-Class Culture and Recent History', in *Higher Education Journal* (Spring 1968).

11. Some of the early projects were described in the *Genealogists' Magazine* (September 1970) and two later ones were screened in October 1971 in the first programme of *History on the Rack*, a B.B.C. 2 television series on history teaching, produced by Felicity Kinross.

Acknowledgments

We would like to express our gratitude to the following teachers and students for contributing reports on their work: Miss Ann Ross and Miss Angela Lythgoe of Fernhill County Primary School, Farnborough, Hants.; Mrs. N.C. Bevan of Meadowvale County Primary School, Bracknell, Berks.; Harry Strongman, Senior Lecturer in History, Berkshire College of Education; Chris Stafford of Maiden Erlegh County Secondary School, Berkshire; Colin Edwards and John Higgs, formerly of Stoneham School, Reading, and Eddie McCall of Garth Hill Comprehensive School, Bracknell.

Thanks are also due to Brendan Murphy, Headmaster of St. Cuthbert's R.C. Primary School, Pemberton, Wigan, for contributing a number of illustrations of Family History work at his school; and to the parents and relatives of pupils in Maiden Erlegh School, Berkshire and Stoneham School, Reading, for allowing the publication of their family information, documents and photographs, and particularly Mrs. E.M. McKinlay who lent us many interesting items. Dr. S. Smith, Headmaster of Stoneham School, Reading, and Mr. E. Martin, Headmaster of Chiltern Edge School, Sonning Common, Oxfordshire, have kindly given permission for the reproduction of work produced by their pupils, and an evening student, Robert Morpeth, has allowed us to reproduce his family documents. We are indebted to Andrew Smith, Brian Hayter and David Hinder of the Department of Educational Technology Berkshire College of Education, for their help with the illustrations.

We also wish to thank Robert Douch, Miss Sheila Savill, Dr. John Fines, Miss Elizabeth Locke and our colleagues Harry Strongman, David and Barbara Stafford and John Chaffer for their helpful comments and suggestions.

The following authors and publishers have kindly allowed us to reproduce copyright material: V.H. Galbraith and C.A. Watts and Co. for the quotation from *An Introduction to the Study of History*; E.A. Wrigley for the quotation from 'Population, Family and Household' in M. Ballard (ed.) *New Movements in the Study and Teaching of History*; P. Fraisse, Eyre and Spottiswoode Ltd., and Harper and Row, Publishers Inc., New York for the extract from *The Psychology of Time*; P. Carpenter for the quotation from *History Teaching, The Era Approach*; Professor R. Hoggart, Chatto and Windus Ltd., and the Oxford University Press, New York, for the extract from *The Uses of Literacy*; The University of London Press Ltd., for the quotations from C.F. Strong, *History in the Secondary School*, and Sir John Adams, *Modern Develop-ments in Educational Practice;* The Schools' Council for the *A Co-operative Programme of Research and Development* and *Working Paper 27, Cross'd with Adversity*; Leslie Smith for the quotations from *Working Papers:* 11, *Society and the Young School Leaver* and 27, *Cross'd with Adversity;* Leslie Smith for the late Evelyn Waugh's *Officers and Gentlemen*; the Controller of H.M. Stationery Office for quotations from the Department of Education and Science's *Parent/Teacher Relations in the Primary School, Education Survey 5.* (1968) and the Ministry of Education pamphlets, *Teaching History* (1952) and *Archives and Education* (1968); the Longman Group, Ltd., for Patrick McGeeney's *Parents are Welcome*; Prof. E.S. Stones for the extract from *An Introduction to Educational Psychology*; Dr. J. Fines for a quotation from 'College of Education Students in the Archives Office', in *Archives* Vol. 9; Peter Prosser of Redlands College, Bristol for a quotation from his article 'Structuring in Curriculum Reform' in *The New Era,* vol. 52, April 1971; the Chandler Publishing Company of San Francisco for a quotation from Asahel D. Woodruff's *Basic Con-cepts of Teaching*; W.H. Laughton and the Cambridge University Press for the quotation from *Teaching About Our People*; Ralph Kitchener of Tewin Wood, Welwyn, Herts., for an extract from his unpublished *Family Saga*; George Ewart Evans and Faber and Faber Ltd., for several extracts from *Where Beards Wag All*; William Heinemann Ltd., and Charles Scribner's Sons, New York, for quotations from John Galsworthy's *The Man of Property*; Routledge and Kegan Paul Ltd., for the extract from Peter Townsend's *The Family Life of Old People*; A.J.P. Taylor for the quotations from *English History 1914-1945* and *The First World War: An Illustrated History;* Sir Isaac Pitman & Sons Ltd., for the quotation from R J. Cruikshank's *Charles Dickens and Early Victorian England*; Ginn and Co. Ltd., for the quotation from E.A. Smith's *A History of the Press* (1970) in their 'Aspects of Social and Economic History' series; Mrs. Molly Harrison for the quotation from *Museum Adventure*; Mrs. Mary Farmer and the Longman Group Ltd., for a quotation from *The Family*; Rupert E. Davies, Principal, Wesley College for a quotation from *Methodism*; Her Majesty's Stationery Office for permission to reproduce birth and marriage certificates and extracts from Census Returns.

We would particularly like to thank our long-suffering publishers for the very personal and friendly treatment we have received. Lastly we must put on record the debt owed to our wives Monica and Pru who not only typed the manuscript innumerable times, but who also tolerated our almost total absence from normal domestic life for several years.

1 AN HISTORICAL ENQUIRY

Certain it is that if the flame of curiosity is to survive the repeated examinations with which, no doubt inevitably, we seek to quench it, it is only possible if historical study from the very beginning is conceived to be a sort of research. The study of history is a personal activity — it is an individual reading the sources of history for himself.

V.H. Galbraith, *An Introduction to the Study of History* (1964), p.61.

THE TEACHER of history is often the victim of unremitting psychological warfare waged by colleagues with better facilities and fatter allowances. The claims of history are, he learns, no longer strong enough to justify its place in the crowded school curriculum. In a scientific and technological age children should be concerned with the world they live in, and with its material, moral and social problems. For the average child up to the school-leaving age, priority should be given to the acquisition of useful skills, rather than the imposition of a premature and heavily diluted academicism inappropriate to his level of conceptual development.

There is much to be said in favour of this view. Many young people leave school abysmally ignorant of their legal rights as citizens, employees, consumers, clients, tenants, patients and parents. Domestic appliances are becoming ever more sophisticated, but a husband is baffled by a trivial fault on the television set and his wife unable to mend a fuse. Even those we label as 'academic' find at college or university that they cannot read widely enough because they have never been taught the skill of speed-reading; they cannot take adequate notes at lectures because they have never learned shorthand. They find the writing of essays and theses unnecessarily laborious because they have never been taught to type. With the strident claims of such important skills unrecognised, how can history hope to survive on the timetable? Clearly we must not only know what to teach and how to teach it, but must have very good reasons for teaching it at all.

The Claims of History

Despite the apparently strong case for abandoning the teaching of history in schools, our whole culture would suffer immeasurably if this drastic step were ever taken on a national scale. The case for history has been cogently stated in numerous works both on the philosophy and on the teaching of history.[1] Briefly the main justifications are:

1. Together with other social studies, history makes it clear to the child that man is more important than the things he discovers or the things he makes even though his existence depends of them.

2. Together with literature, geography and art, it enlarges the child's sympathy and stimulates his imagination by giving him vicarious experiences radically different from those of his everyday life. Do we want a world where a child is mentally incapable of widening his horizons beyond the perimeter of his housing estate?

3. Together with the natural and social sciences, it trains the child in the gathering, sifting and evaluation of evidence. Such a training was never more necessary than in a society in which mass media can make children and adults the passive recipients of the carefully manipulated thought-packs of politicians, advertisers, planners and bureaucrats.

4. Only history can provide the basis for an understanding of *time* through the perception of *change*, thus setting the present into a broad continuum of past, present and future. The present depends upon the past and in its turn influences the future. Perhaps it is a lack of perception of his place in time that allows 20th-century man selfishly and prodigally to squander natural resources it has taken millions of years to accumulate and uncritically to assume that what is new is, *ipso facto*, better.

5. Perhaps most important of all, by providing some insight into societies, cultures and values that differ from our own, history gives us a frame of reference within which we may understand ourselves better, and distinguish the permanent influences on human behaviour and values from those very much determined by time and place. In what ways do we resemble our ancestors and to what extent do we differ from them?

The principal claim of history to a place on the school timetable therefore lies in the help it can give children to come to a better understanding of themselves and their cultural, moral, religious and social assumptions, through their study of the thoughts and behaviour of men and women in the past.

Why is it often so Boring?

Important though these claims are, they rarely seem to have been realised in our schools, particularly at the secondary stage. For many pupils, history is little more than a twice weekly exhumation of bare, lifeless bones which would be much more decently left undisturbed. In Mary Price's words, 'There are the strongest reasons for supposing that in a great many schools it is excruciatingly, dangerously, dull and what is more, of little apparent relevance to the pupils'.[2]

Part of the fault undoubtedly lies in the examination system. This has a desiccating and demoralising effect on history teaching, not only because most examinations still put a premium on memory, but also because they over-emphasise one aspect of history (the political) and one unit (the nation state) at the expense of others. More damning still, the periods set are usually far too long for the intensive study which alone can provide historical insight, and the examination questions demand precise 'answers' — which even scholars hesitate to advance. Such examinations encourage the use and proliferation of textbooks written in generalised terms, in which all but the most eminent individuals are reduced to abstractions: the poor, the rich, the mob, the gentry, Catholics and Protestants, Whigs and Tories, and sometimes, as in, 'the bill passed its second reading after a stormy passage' there is no reference to agents at all. Most of such textbooks are at least two removes from the evidence on which they are based, and, despite the fact that more and more facsimiles of primary sources are available, the National Secretary of the Students' Action Union expressed the feelings of many children when he complained:

> At the moment, people are given text-books which are the work of historians, so you get the fixed ideas of 20 or 30 years ago — how they thought of, say, the nineteenth century. Why can't we see reproductions of actual documents and statistics of the time, the things historians use themselves when they are researching for a book? Instead, we only get what they managed to find out, and what they saw fit to use. Nor do we ever see the facts they reject. We want to approach history exactly as historians. do.[3]

However, we are being less than honest if we make examinations the scapegoat for our failure.[4] Even if we have to acknowledge their hegemony, they need not dominate our teaching until the tenth year of schooling. The fact is that history teachers have become ensnared in a tradition which is so strong that only a minority are willing or able to break with it. This tradition is now worn out, and must be replaced by one which bases its claims not upon a received corpus of emasculated academic knowledge, but upon the needs of children who will be adults in the 21st century.

The prospect would be depressing enough if much history teaching were only dull, irrelevant, dehumanised and second-hand. Alas, for many children it is actually incomprehensible. Researchers[5] have confirmed what perceptive teachers have suspected for at least half a century — that schoolchildren may use abstract social and political terms correctly but such terms 'stand in their minds for no clear ideas whatsoever'.[6] Most teachers aim their lessons beyond the children's conceptual ability, not recognising that it is impossible to teach history successfully to the average child with methods not dissimilar to those used in the sixth form and the university. Hence the children's boredom.

History teachers today must strive to further not only intellectual growth, but emotional and social growth as well. In the realisation of these aims, many different varieties of history, from Family History to World History have a role to play. What will not find a place will be the useless and boring regurgitation of dates and battles, causes and effects, acts and treaties.

Re-appraising the Tradition: The Child-centred Approach

The need for a radical re-appraisal of the tradition has been an oft recurring theme of educationalists. In 1904, Mary S. Barnes saw history as 'not much longer destined to sleep while little books and dogmatic teachers tell weary souls what history was and did'.[7] The activity methods developed in Primary schools have clearly demonstrated that the involvement of the child in what he is doing is the crucial factor in learning, and, after a long line of unheeded prophets,[8] there are signs at last that teachers are becoming converted to the dictum that 'for children, history is initially a process of relating the past to their direct experiences'.[9] Motivation derives from interest, and interest in its turn comes from an obvious relevance to the child's daily life.

Teaching History Backwards

Preoccupied with the actualities of his immediate present, the young child ignores the affairs of the wider world and of the past; but, inevitably, there comes a time when he begins to reflect about himself and his origins.[10] Thus, on psychological grounds, there seems very good reason for starting the study of history with the child himself in his immediate present, helping him to create a coherent model of his way of life, and then to consider, first, the lives of his parents and grandparents and, eventually, those of his more remote ancestors.

This principle of studying history backwards is well illustrated by Marc Bloch's vivid metaphor of the historian examining a film of which only the last picture is clear. In order to reconstruct the faded features of the others, he is forced to unwind the spool in the opposite direction from that in which the pictures were taken.[11]

The Basic Social Unit

The corollary to moving backwards in time is moving outwards into ever larger social groups. In the last analysis, society is only a collection of individuals, and our educational system rightly emphasises the development of the individual personality. Aron suggests the 'Self' — the individual who interests one most — as a reasonable starting point for a study of history which then moves through various stages towards an understanding of man's collective past. 'Historical knowledge', he says, 'must be considered as the extension of the knowledge of self and of others'.[12]

Aron's programme, however, highlights an interesting gap in historical literature and teaching. Unlike sociologists and anthropologists, few historians or history teachers have given any overt recognition to the fact that the fundamental social unit is the family.[13] Yet in studying the history of the family, the individual comes much closer to an understanding of the foundations of history than he does by studying either Local or National History. In the family, man learns 'attitudes of mind, modes of conduct, ideals and taboos', which he will later pass on to his own children:

> If the criterion of the importance of a theme to history is the proportion of the population it involves, and its centrality to other historical themes, then the history of the family need fear few rivals.[14]

Family History is the essential missing link in the chain of Biography, Local, National and World History. But, looking at ever larger units involves the risk of increased abstraction and generalisation. Some teachers may therefore prefer to treat Family History as the hub where Local, National and World History all meet in individual family experiences of changing beliefs and values, of slumps and booms, of emigration, colonial service, overseas trade and of war. Although Wrigley has stressed this 'strategic position' of the family in social, economic and political studies, we would emphasise that Family History does not exist merely as the servant of other varieties of history. It has intrinsic importance and interest.[15]

The Oldest Variety of History

It is not surprising to find that, just as the family is the oldest and most basic unit of society, so is Family History the ancestor and root of all other forms of historical enquiry. In primitive societies the only 'history' was the collective memory of 'the ancestors', the time-scale was provided by their names, and this real or fictitious common genealogy provided the unifying link of the community,[16] points which have not escaped the notice of educationalists stressing the necessity for the child's personal involvement in his studies.[17]

Sociological research has shown that for relatively stable rural communities, Family History is still the only history that matters.

Bernot and Blancard made a study of a French village in Normandy where two different populations co-existed, one of peasants who had been rooted for generations in the same soil, the other of glass blowers recruited from other provinces of France. The results were interesting:

> The peasant lives in a duration which is that of his family, and his recollections go back beyond his own personal memories. 'This land was bought by his grandfather, this building was constructed by his father;' . . . The glass-blower for his part is an immigrant, cut off from his ancestors and their work. Perhaps they were workers like him and never had roots in one place or one home. Once he has been transplanted into a new region, his own memories of his youth and childhood do not attach themselves to the new background. He is almost without a past.[18]

N.B.:

Here we have in microcosm, agrarian and industrial man, the one with a past that is alive and meaningful; the other cut off from his agrarian heritage and with no fresh tradition to take its place. The de-racinated glassblowers of Nouville stand as representatives of the millions of children in growing industrial cities or anonymous housing estates. Before one can hope to interest such children in the past, one must restore to them the family roots of which industrialisation has robbed them. As Sir Anthony Wagner has observed,[19] the post-war boom in genealogy[20] has undoubtedly been produced by this feeling of rootlessness in urban man and his longing for a past. Just as all history has grown out of the genealogies, family histories and tribal legends of primitive man, so can children become deeply involved in the past only if they feel kinship with their ancestors.

A Training in Historical Method

Family History satisfies the demands of modern educational philosophy and pyschology. It provides a type of enquiry which is both relevant, in that it starts with the child's own life and interests, and comprehensible because it deals with a span of time and size of unit which he can readily grasp. It thus presents a vivid contrast to traditional history, where, says Butterfield, 'we start with an abridged story, seen in the round and constructed out of what in reality are broad generalizations'. He observes that, whereas the teacher of mathematics starts 'on the hard earth', teaching the simplest things first, the history teacher paradoxically starts 'in the clouds at the very top of the highest skyscraper'. Only the research student, says Butterfield, is able genuinely to establish the assertions which he makes.[21] Butterfield does not, however, seem to have envisaged the possibility that this paradox might be resolved through a classroom revolution in which teachers, refusing to accept any longer the Divine Right of the traditional canon, depose it in favour of a different kind of school history — one which enables the child to handle and think about the main categories of evidence used by the professional historian.

Many children, taught by traditional methods, leave school with the conviction that there exists a huge pile of historical 'facts' from which the writers of history books try to dig out those they consider the most important. If such children think at all about the writing of history, they probably rate it as low-grade hack-work, in which all you need to do is choose which facts to leave out of your book. This delusion is reinforced by many historical projects. Children, rightly, see something artificial in pursuing a so-called enquiry, to which better brains than theirs have already discovered all the answers. Following 'a path that has already been well-trodden',[22] all they have to do is decide which facts they are going to transfer from books to their own folders.

N.B

A Unique and Original Enquiry

In a Family History scheme, the investigation is a completely original one. Children learn how to search for evidence by being introduced to many different sources of information: oral evidence, family papers, such as birth, marriage and death certificates, letters, and diaries, photographs, and, in some cases, local and national records such as parish registers and census returns. In order to make sense of what they have gleaned from these sources, the children will be driven to consult reference books and may be guided to use local libraries and museums and to write to more distant ones for information. Such enquiries will help them to realise the extent and relative value of the sources available to the historian.

The information they discover may prompt them to ask fresh questions about facets of life in the past that had not struck them before. They can be taught to check their information before using it as the starting point for further enquiry, and thus learn the importance of verifying evidence. They will find that accuracy and precision are as necessary in history as they are in mathematics, technical drawing or science, and, like all historians, having discovered and verified their material, the pupils will then have to record it and will be faced with problems of organisation and presentation.

In a Family History scheme, the child writes a lengthy and detailed piece of work using as many types of evidence as possible. As Carpenter stresses,

> The application to detail is necessary, not only in order to do justice to history as a subject, but to fill a psychological need. It satisfies a child's natural curiosity and confronts him with something manageable which, when he has mastered it, gives a sense of satisfaction and achievement. In his own particular field, he will be the acknowledged authority, and his classmates will respect him as such.[23]

One of the strongest arguments for Family History is that it is the only variety of history where the child is not only an authority, but can be a unique authority, an idea which has great appeal for children. He is encouraged to acquire background information not because he is told it is 'important', but because it is relevant to his particular family. He is involved in looking for and selecting relevant material and in developing his own criteria of historical importance. At the same time, however, he acquaints himself with the kind of social, economic and cultural information that he would encounter in a straightforward patch study of, for example, Edwardian England or the Second World War, and the teacher will need to devise ways of showing how generalisations are made from a multitude of individual experiences. However, it cannot be emphasised enough that the primary aim is for the child to engage in an historical enquiry which is comparable, at his own level, with that undertaken by the professional historian. He is not merely collecting data which illustrates national themes, a false emphasis which is a perpetual temptation to the secondary school teacher with a syllabus to cover.

Re-living the Past

Although there is a powerful case for introducing children to historical method, many teachers lay greater stress on 'feeding the imagination'. They believe that the function of history is to increase the child's understanding of life, by laying bare the way previous generations lived, felt and thought. The pupils must 'live in imagination in conditions different from their own and must think out how these conditions would affect life'.[24] Such a pursuit of vicarious experience need not, however, exclude training in historical method. The two should be seen as opposite sides of the same coin, and Family History is an ideal medium not only for introducing children to the skills of the historian but for immersing them in the past.

The dramatic impact of seeing events through the eyes of one family has long been appreciated by novelists and dramatists, and the popular appeal of such an approach has been shown by the enthusiastic reception given to television productions such as *The Forsyte Saga* and *A Family at War*. It is interesting to note that real-life Family History, such as *The First Churchills* and *The Six Wives of Henry VIII*, has proved equally compulsive viewing.

However, despite the power of a family saga in the form of a novel or a television play, rarely is its potential exploited in the classroom. With the exception of Katherine Moore's *Family Fortunes: A Story of Social Change*, even the technique of following a fictitious family over several generations has not been used in history text and topic books.

A Living History Lab.

Some teachers, whilst readily accepting the idea of studying the family fortunes of Henry VIII or the Churchills, might argue that a child's researches into his own family history over the last few generations are not really 'history', since they deal with the recent past and the leading roles are taken not by kings, ministers, civil servants and generals, but by people whose names rarely appear in the most exhaustive historical accounts.

The strength of the case for studying recent history lies not in its greater relevance to contemporary problems, but in the fact that, during the lifetimes of men and women in their 70s, 80s and 90s, there have been more technological, scientific, economic, and social changes than in the whole previous history of mankind. Thus the last hundred years will provide a laboratory in which children can learn about the past. As Toynbee once dryly observed, 'One's contemporaries are the only people whom one can ever catch alive'. An emphasis on the near past brings 'history' close enough to impress the child with its actuality.

The Dynamics of Social Change

It is important not only that children should be helped to reach an imaginative understanding of the past, but also that they should be given an insight into the dynamics of social change. These are well illustrated by the movement of our ancestors from one environment to another and, most particularly in the last century, by their movement from the country to towns. This process of urbanisation is exemplified in Richard Hoggart's family history:

> My grandmother married a cousin and at that time their family was still rural, living in a village about a dozen miles from Leeds. Sometime in the seventies she and her young husband were drawn to that expanding city, into the service of the steel-works on the south side. She set about raising a growing family — ten were born but some were 'lost' — in the vast new brick acres of Hunslet. All over the North and Midlands the same thing was happening, the villages losing their young people, the towns staining the countryside around with raw cheap housing. They were insufficiently provided with medical, educational and other social facilities; their streets, inadequately cleansed and lighted, were being packed with families whose pattern of life was still to a large extent rural. Many died young (the plaque commemorating a cholera epidemic used still to stand in a railway shunting-yard that I passed each day on my way to the secondary school); 'T.B.' took a heavy toll.
>
> My grandmother lived through all this and on through the First World War until almost the beginning of the Second; she learned to become a city-dweller. Yet in every line of her body and in many of her attitudes her country background spoke. Her house, still rented at nine shillings a week in 1939, was never truly urban. Newspaper packets of home-dried herbs hung from the scullery ceiling; a pot of goose-grease lay always on the shelf there,

in case anyone 'got a bad chest'. She retained in the vitality of her spirit, in the vigour of her language, in the occasional peasant quality of her humour, a strength which her children had not and towards which they had at times something of a sophisticated and urbanized 'neshness' (soft squeamishness). She called you a 'corf-eerd' (calf-head) without any conscious sarcasm; she was full of pithy aphorisms, such as 't'owd cock crows, t'yung un larns' (of a cheeky boy whose mother did not control him); she had a wealth of supersitious tags and old remedies to fall upon in emergencies . . .

For our family she was a first-generation townswoman and therefore only partly a townswoman. Meanwhile the second generation, her children, were growing up. They were growing up from the time of the Third Reform Act, through the series of Education Acts, the various Housing Acts, the Factory Acts and Public Health Acts, through the Boer War; and the youngest was just old enough to serve in the First World War. The boys went to 'Board' school and so into steelworks or, since we had white-collar leanings, into the more genteel openings, as grocery assistants or salesmen in town shops, though this was regarded as almost a step up in class. The girls were swallowed one after the other into the always-demanding, because always-changing, population of tailoresses, those girls who were and are the foundation of Leeds' predominance as a centre for ready-made clothing.[25]

Some family histories illustrate even more dramatic changes in environment — movements from one country to another. Children are fascinated by the stories of emigrant relatives and also by those of ex-soldiers, sailors, civil servants, doctors and engineers who have served abroad. In some cases children in the class have themselves experienced a much more dramatic change than that of the 19th-century Hoggarts. If the other pupils in the class can come to understand the difficulties of their own migrant ancestors, they may also begin to appreciate the cultural shock experienced by many contemporary immigrants.

*   *   *

Through its emphasis firstly on the slow and carefully structured way in which the child is introduced to historical time and to social groupings, secondly on the relevance, uniqueness and originality of the child's own enquiry, and thirdly on the vicarious experience of the past through the use of a 'living history laboratory', Family History can do something which traditional methods of history teaching have so far failed to do. We are not just proposing a more interesting way of tackling traditional content. We strike at the root of a history syllabus which is content-based and bring forward for the consideration of teachers a way in which children can study history so as to acquire not merely a knowledge of factual events and incidents, but also what J.S. Bruner has called the essential 'structure' of a subject, that is, 'the skills and techniques that can transfer to further study, and a maturing concept of what the subject is about'.[26]

Notes and References

1   *See*, for example: A. Marwick, *The Nature of History* (1970), pp.12-19; G.R. Elton, *The Practice of History* (1967), pp.67-69; P.H.J.H. Gosden and D.W. Sylvester, *History for the Average Child* (1968), pp.1-7.

2   M. Price, 'History in Danger', in *History*, vol. 53, no. 179 (October 1968), p.344. *See also*: M. Booth, *History Betrayed* (1969), pp.59-67. On pupils' reactions, *see*, for example, *Schools Council Enquiry 1* (1969); Edward Blishen (ed.), *The Schools We Would Like* (1969), pp.55-77.

3   Interview reported by Jill Tweedie in *The Guardian*, 7 September 1970, p.9.

4   For effective refutations of the examination as scapegoat *see*: Eric C. Walker, *History Teaching for Today* (1935), pp.33-36; D. Thompson and J. Reeves, *The Quality of Education* (1947), pp.125-136. The weight of conservatism comes rather from the teachers than from the examiners.

5   *See*, for example: F.A. Peel, *The Pupil's Thinking* (1960), pp.114, 121-124, 126-130; W.H. Burston and D. Thompson, *Studies in the Nature and Teaching of History* (1967), pp.159-190; Jeanette Coltham, 'Junior School Children's Understanding of Some Terms Commonly Used in the Teaching of History', unpublished Ph.D. thesis, Manchester University (1960); R.N. Hallam, 'An Investigation into some aspects of the historical thinking of children and adolescents', unpublished M.Ed. thesis Leeds University (1966); 'Logical Thinking in History', *Educational Review*, vol. 19 no. 3 (1967); 'Piaget and Thinking in History', in M. Ballard (ed.) *New Movements in the Study and Teaching of History* (1970); 'Piaget and the Teaching of History', *Educational Research*, vol. 12 no. 1 (1969), pp.3-12; H. Bell, 'The Logical Thinking of Children in Primary Schools when learning History', unpublished M.Ed. thesis, Reading University (1964); S.K. Stones, 'Factors Influencing the capacity of Adolescents to think in abstract terms in the understanding of History', unpublished M.Ed. thesis, Manchester University (1967).

6   C. Firth, *The Learning of History in Elementary Schools* 2nd ed. (1932), p.101.

7   Mary S. Barnes, *Studies in Historical Method* (Boston, Mass., 1904), p.44.

8   Notably F. Clarke, *Foundations of History Teaching* (1929); J.J. Findlay, *History and its Place in Education* (1923); J.J. Bell, *History in School: A method book* (1945).

9   Leo J. Alilunas, 'The Problem of Children's Historical Mindedness', in J.S. Roucek (ed.), *The Teaching of History* (1968), p.192.

10 *See*, P. Cressot, 'L'Histoire et la Psychologie de L'Enfant', in P. Josserand (ed.), *L'Enseignement de L'Histoire*, Paris (1957), p.14.

11 M. Bloch, *The Historian's Craft*, (English translation 1954), p.46.

12 R. Aron, *Introduction to the Philosophy of History*, (English translation, George Irwin, 1961), p.48.

13   Important exceptions to this generalisation are the historical demo-
      graphers, such as Laslett and Wrigley, and the pioneering historians of
      childhood, Philippe Aries, Ivy Pinchbeck and Margaret Hewitt.

14   E.A.Wrigley,'Population, Family and Household' in M. Ballard, *New
      Movements in the Study and Teaching of History*(1970), p.93.

15   Its value has also been emphasised by P. Mathias. *See* his 'Economic
      History — Direct and Oblique' in M. Ballard, *op.cit.*, pp.89-90.

16   S. Toulmin and J. Goodfield, *The Discovery of Time* (1965), p.26.

17   P.H.J.H. Gosden and D.W. Sylvester, *op.cit.*, p.5.

18   L. Bernot and R. Blanchard, *Nouville, un village francais*, Paris:
      Institut d'Ethnologie. (1953), cited in P. Fraisse, *The Psychology of
      Time*, English translation. (1964), pp.169-170.

19   *English Ancestry* (1961), p.6.

20   The membership of the Society of Genealogists has gone up from about
      650 in 1948 to well over 3,000 in 1972. Almost all the numerous do-it-
      yourself genealogical manuals have been written since 1953. Other
      indications of the growing interest in genealogy are the organisation of
      adult courses and conferences on Family History by University Extra-
      Mural Boards and Evening Institutes and the commercial marketing of
      an *Ancestors* kit.

21   H. Butterfield, *History and Human Relations* (1951), p.168.

22   John Fairley, *Patch History and Creativity* (1970), p.32. Fairley insists,
      'if history teaching is to mean anything in a truly educational sense, then
      it must concern itself primarily with historical method', defined as, 'a
      search for evidence, the collation of selected material and the presenta-
      tion of results and conclusions', but, like most of his predecessors, he
      recoils from the full implications of his own premises, for he sees the
      child not as 'seeking out his sources', but as following a 'well-trodden
      path'.

23   P. Carpenter, *History Teaching, The Era Approach* (1964), p.42.

24   J. Welton, *The Psychology of Education* (1911), p.64.

25   R. Hoggart, *The Uses of Literacy*, Pelican edn. (1958), p.viii.

26   J.S. Bruner, *The Process of Education* (Cambridge Mass., 1960), pp.6-8;
      17-32.

2 AN INTERDISCIPLINARY PROJECT

If we fail to co-ordinate, wherever possible, the work of one,
subject with that of the others in the curriculum, we shall get
less than the full value out of each subject by itself and of the
educational process as a whole.

C.F. Strong, *History in the Primary School*
1950, p.39.

AS THE SCHOOLS' COUNCIL has pointed out, although the
main and long-term challenge to teachers of history is to make their
subject meaningful and attractive in its own right, they should also
be concerned 'about the part history can play in interdisciplinary
and problem-orientated work'.[1] However, 'interdisciplinary' is used
in so many senses, describes so many methods of organisation and
embraces so many degrees of collaboration between subject
specialists, that it is worth examining briefly some of the ways in
which teachers interpret the term, the respective merits and weaknesses of such interpretations, and the possible roles of Family
History in such work.

Ancillary Service: At the most elementary level, the history
teacher draws upon the techniques and materials used by his colleagues. For example, in a lesson on the American Civil War, he
may outline the main geographical features which determined the
causes and course of the conflict. In a study of the Industrial
Revolution, he may draw graphs to depict the growth of British
trade in relation to that of other European countries. During a lesson on the 18th century, he may play a piece of Haydn to evoke
the atmosphere of a firmly established social order and its classical
sense of form. Thus he makes geography, mathematics and music
the servants of history.

Co-operation: At this level, instead of talking about the
geographical features of America, he may ask the geography
specialist to come and give the lesson, while he takes his colleague's
geography lesson on, say, the Growth of London. This time, the
lesson on the background to the American Civil War will stress
geographical rather than historical features. The children are more
likely to learn about the climatic factors which moulded the
economy of the South than about the position of Gettysburg,
which is significant for historical rather than geographical reasons.
Meanwhile, in his lesson on the Growth of London, the historian
may give as much emphasis to the part the metropolis has played
in the political history of England as to its central role in the
economy. Ideally, the two specialists work in co-operative partner-

ship in the same classroom. Through such co-operation the children are taught that there are different ways of looking at the same information.

Co-ordination: Here the history and geography teachers devise syllabuses which have deliberately planned points of contact, so that while the history master is teaching the American Civil War, his colleague is teaching the geography of the United States. At this level, the children are looking at America through two pairs of spectacles, not just in one lesson, but over a fairly long period. The English specialist might be persuaded to contribute by discussing scenes from Drinkwater's *Abraham Lincoln.* At the end of the term, the two or three teachers may even collaborate in a joint examination paper which asks questions such as:

> To what extent was the course of the American Civil War determined by geographical factors?

or

> Do you think that John Drinkwater's portrayal of Abraham Lincoln was historically accurate?

Integration: The most sophisticated level of interdisciplinary work is where the children are not even aware of crossing the disciplinary frontiers. Here historical, geographical, and literary studies are integrated under an umbrella title such as *American Studies* or *War.*

In *Working Paper No. 11,* the Schools' Council includes among the fundamental characteristics of teaching of common concern to all teachers, the belief that the child 'must have some measure of intellectual extension so that he can begin to comprehend the complexity and totality of man's civilisation and environment'. It suggests that

> the ultimate goal is an integrated syllabus in the humanities, not in order to create a new subject of doubtful parentage, but to lay all the old subjects and many of the newer disciplines under tribute to answer real questions in which the pupils can be interested.[2]

More recently, the Schools' Council's *Integrated Studies Project* at Keele for the 11-16 age group, directed by David Bolam, has defined 'integration' as:

> exploration of any theme, area, or problem which requires the help of more than one school subject for its full understanding, and the interest of more than one teacher in achieving this.

He points out that integration must have a double concern: 'the co-operative use of subjects and co-operation between teachers to make this possible'.[3]

Interdisciplinary Enquiry: A very different way of looking at interdisciplinary work is suggested by the Goldsmith's College

Curriculum Laboratory, whose members have argued a strong case for a radically different approach to the curriculum — an approach based on Interdisciplinary Enquiry (I.D.E.):

> Specialist teachers' knowledge and skills are best deployed in secondary schooling if they are directed for at least part of the curriculum to a shared attempt to explore problems of fundamental importance to young people and to adults: to these the answers are necessarily interdisciplinary.[4]

At first sight this may seem indistinguishable from the aim of the Schools' Council's Integrated Projects. However, the I.D.E. lobby criticises all integrated studies projects as being 'devised as closed systems prepared for handling by a class teacher'. Edward Mason comments that

> the more of such schemes a school goes in for, the more rigidly its time-tabling for class teaching is determined by the need to carry out the instructions on the packet,[5]

a sweeping generalisation which nonetheless provides us with a salutary and timely note of warning.

By comparison with other integrative projects, in I.D.E. the content appears to be almost wholly unstructured. After a 'lift off', the children explore problems in small collaborative groups, picking their own paths through the fields of human knowledge or engaging in practical activities. Free to consult whenever they wish with a 'focus' group of teachers, they can go where they will: the enquiry is completely open-ended and the teachers are advisers, not directors. However, it must be emphasised that the Goldsmith's College team see I.D.E. as only one strand in a fourfold curriculum which also includes: autonomous studies (i.e. skills to meet predicted needs); special interest studies (children and teachers with common interests gather together); and remedial studies (overcoming stumbling blocks to children's progress).

The prophetic fervour of Interdisciplinarianism has made it the most rapidly expanding of all the educational sects. Yet not all history teachers are willing to accept a development which they see as an attack on 'academic standards', an adulteration of subject-matter and a serious threat to their professional autonomy. 'Integrated studies has become the new shibboleth, and those who express doubt are branded as reactionary', bemoans Ballard.[6] Whilst recognizing that there are many areas for fruitful co-operation, he expresses grave doubts about artificial mergers. Thus many history teachers, like Ballard, are quite happy to borrow skills from other disciplines where they are useful and to invite the co-operation of other colleagues. For the most part they draw the line after co-operation and before co-ordination. Referring specifically to the relationship between the historian and the geographer, Ballard comments that 'as soon as the link becomes all important, both teachers lose their freedom of choice'.[7] Much the same point of view has been expressed by Roy Wake, the Staff Inspector for History.[8] Some historians have similar reservations about university integrated courses. They are 'superb in intention, but in practice a bit wet round the bottom', comments Marwick.[9]

Yet history has a more important role in interdisciplinary work than most other school subjects, for it is not simply a record of events but also the story of how man's thinking and knowledge has evolved. It embraces every other subject in the past, and, because of its involvement in man's psychology and social behaviour, must concern itself with contemporary life and issues. Thus history is the natural focal point for work in many subjects, and the reason why it is often taught more interestingly at the Primary level may be that there the teachers are not history specialists. The history they teach is, therefore, more related to other areas of human knowledge and, above all, is concerned not with parties, policies and the balance of power, but with people.

The contrasts between Primary and Secondary Schools are now marked. In recent years, the Primary Schools increasingly have stressed individualised and enquiry-based topic work, which, inevitably transcends subject boundaries, as the children are encouraged to explore themes relevant to their growing awareness of the world around them. The Secondary Schools are still much more subject conscious. Too often the pupil's intellectual diet has been dictated, not by his needs, even considered in the broadest and most liberal sense, but by what has always been assumed to be the essential content of the subject. Thus, in our *laissez-faire* educational system some history teachers have been more preoccupied with teaching history than with educating children; but, as John Holt has acidly commented,

> The idea of the 'body of knowledge', to be picked up at school and used for the rest of one's life, is nonsense in a world as complicated and rapidly changing as ours.[10]

Children need to be prepared for three roles: as individuals who will have to cope with a complex network of human relationships; as future citizens with a vital part to play in a democratic society; and as future workers whose minds must be sufficiently flexible to cope with ever changing demands upon their talents and skills.

How often does the specialist in the Secondary School pause to consider what part he can play in achieving these aims? Convinced of the unique importance of his own subject, and complaining bitterly that the headmaster is so purblind as to give him only two periods a week per class, he hardly ever sees himself as a member of a team concerned with the totality of the child's educational experience. Thus the cart is put firmly before the horse and the driver is blinkered, a situation in which subject boundaries can be crossed only by accident or subterfuge, and even then the driver looks for the quickest way to back the cart on to his own territory.

This might not be so disastrous if the terrain was as recognisable as it used to be. Alas, the floods of academic research driven on by the winds of change have breached the dikes, swept away many familiar boundary marks and reduced much of the territory to a quagmire. The history teacher is bewildered by the competing claims of political, economic and social history; the rival strident voices of the World History faction telling him to use a telescope and those of the Local Historians (not to mention the Family Historians!) telling him to use a microscope; the 'methodologists' stressing that method is all that matters, and the 'reanimationists' insinuating that it is alright as long as the children 'can relive a period' through drama, creative writing, painting and modelling.

The imaginative reconstruction of the past, must, of its very nature, be interdisciplinary, and children should be encouraged to express themselves in prose and poetry, art and drama. However, to say that Family History is by nature interdisciplinary and leave it at that is not enough. If the history teacher declares for an isolationist policy, calling in the rest of the staff only when he wants to trade with them, interdisciplinary work is likely to suffer the fate of the League of Nations without the United States.

In most of the experimental secondary school projects so far undertaken Family History has steered the middle path between isolation and integration. It has provided a base from which raids have been made into the territories of other subjects.

Although Family History projects necessarily involve creative writing, art and drama and may involve mathematics or even mechanics (see page 159) they have been conceived mainly in historical terms, which may not satisfy the aims of teachers of other subjects. However, Environmental History, (i.e. Family History combined with Local History), may well supply a starting point for such an integrated curriculum in history, geography and social science and in our projected Branching Programme Book, *Crossing the Frontiers*, we hope to show how Family History can be combined with sociological work on the Family as an institution to produce a viable integrated scheme.

In the present volume we seek merely to indicate Family History's potential at the levels of ancillary service, co-operation and co-ordination. Even these modest levels of interdisciplinary activity require fairly radical changes in the content and organisation of the curriculum. At present many history teachers are reluctant to press art, drama and modelling into ancillary service, partly because of lack of space and materials, but primarily because of the conservative tradition in Secondary Schools which frowns upon any innovation which upsets the carefully planned fragmentation of the child's working day into seven, precisely labelled 40-minute compartments.

There is an urgent need for a systematic exploration of the reasons why co-operation with the English, art, drama or domestic science teacher may be desirable and how it may be practicable, of how methods, ideas, subject matter and even syllabuses may be run parallel or co-ordinated, of what changes may be necessary in the school's organisation, of how joint assessments may be made of the children's work. At present the situation in Secondary Schools is so confused that no generally applicable advice can be offered as to how in a Family History scheme links may best be formed with other subjects and how they may then be exploited. However, the following suggestions may be found helpful.

English

It is with English that Family History has the closest links. Literature, imaginative writing and the more functional side of English are basic to the success of the project. For this reason a Family History scheme is perhaps best run by the history and English teachers in conjunction, calling upon the specialist skills of other members of staff as required.

In order to re-create the past, children will need to supplement their relatives' memories, photographs and mementoes with excerpts from autobiographies and novels. Though too difficult in their entirety for most children, such memoirs as Laurie Lee's *Cider With Rosie*, Richard Church's *Over the Bridge* and Spike Mays's *Reuben's Corner* will supply an abundance of vivid extracts suitable for most age groups. The same is true of many adult novels. For example, most teachers would agree that Evelyn Waugh's *Officers and Gentlemen* is unsuitable for younger children. Consider, however, the following evocative passage concerning the evacuation of the British Army from Crete:

> The quay was littered with abandoned equipment and the wreckage of bombardment. Among the scrap and waste stood a pile of rations — bully beef and biscuit — and a slow-moving concourse of soldiers foraging. Sergeant Smiley pushed his way through them and passed back half a dozen tins. There was a tap of fresh water running to waste in the wall of a ruined building. Guy and his section filled their bottles, drank deep, refilled them, turned off the tap, then breakfasted. The little town was burned, battered and deserted by its inhabitants. The ghosts of an army teemed everywhere. Some were quite apathetic, too weary to eat; others were smashing their rifles on the stones, taking a fierce relish in this symbolic farewell to their arms; an officer stamped on his binoculars; a motor-bike was burning; there was a small group under command of a sapper captain doing something to a seedy-looking fishing-boat that lay on its side, out of the water, on the beach. One man sat on the sea-wall methodically stripping down his Bren and throwing the parts separately far into the scum.[11]

With a few difficult words explained, this passage could be used by most 11-year olds. Many school libraries are crammed with the unread novels of Dickens, Hardy and H.G. Wells, and if they are not, second-hand copies of the works of such Victorian and Edwardian authors can be bought very cheaply. Here is a passage from Charles Kingsley's *Alton Locke*, again not a book many children could be persuaded to read in its entirety.

> We trudged on, over wide stubbles, with innumerable weeds; over wide fallows, in which the deserted ploughs stood frozen fast; then over clover and grass burnt black with frost; then over a field of turnips, where we passed a large fold of hurdles, within which some hundred sheep stood, with their heads turned from the cutting blast. All was dreary, idle, silent; no sound or sign of human beings. One wondered where the people lived, who cultivated so vast a tract of civilised, over-peopled, nineteenth-century England. As we came up to the fold, two little boys hailed us from the inside — two little wretches with blue noses and white cheeks, scarecrows of rags and patches, their feet peeping through bursten shoes twice too big for them, who seemed to have shared between them a ragged pair of worsted gloves, and cowered among the sheep, under the shelter of a hurdle, crying and inarticulate with cold.
> 'What's the matter, boys?'
> 'Turmits is froze, and us can't turn the handle of the cutter. Do ye gie us a turn, please?'
> We scrambled over the hurdles, and gave the miserable little creatures the benefit of ten minutes' labour. They seemed too small for such exertion: their little hands were purple with chilblains, and they were so sorefooted they could scarcely limp. I was surprised to find them at least three years older than their size and looks denoted, and still more surprised, too, to find that their salary for all this bitter exposure to the elements — such as I believe I could not have endured two days running — was the vast sum of one shilling a week each, Sundays included. 'They didn't never go to school, nor to church nether, except just now and then, sometimes — they had to mind the shep.'
> I went on, sickened with the contrast between the highly-bred over-fed, fat, thick-woolled animals, with their troughs of turnips and malt-dust, and their racks of rich clover-hay, and their little pent-house of rock-salt, having nothing to do but to eat and sleep, and eat again, and the little half-starved shivering animals who were their slaves.[12]

Valuable though such passages are in helping to recreate the past, reading is not enough. All learning should be active, and the reading must be supplemented by imaginative writing.

John Fines laments the shallow base of much that is termed 'creative writing':

> Children are urged to 'express themselves', when they have pathetically little experience to express, and to be 'creative' when there is nothing with which they can create.

N.B.

He stresses that history can provide sufficient imaginative stimulus for every child.[13] In a Family History project, this may be a great uncle's voyage to Australia in 1905 or Grandfather's involvement in the General Strike. Most of this will be expressed in prose, but occasionally the opportunity will present itself for the children to write poetry. This kind of assignment can bring out a feeling for the past which is usually totally lacking in the traditional essay, an adult and highly academic form of communication, totally unsuited to 90% of the children in our schools. For example, a class which is studying the Second World War may be asked for homework to write a short account of 'life on the Home Front'. There are two main reasons why this may produce neither a very active nor a very informed response. Firstly, the child is being asked to work at a very high level of generalisation; secondly, the traditional essay form usually deals with facts and highly impersonal judgments rather than with personal responses to situations. The average child may find the task an arid one, and even if he has been asked to talk to parents and relatives, he may find that he can get an uncongenial homework completed more quickly if he copies out a couple of paragraphs from a textbook. This may also conform more closely to his idea of what 'history' is.

However, there are alternatives. One is to break the task down into a series of imaginative reconstructions. The child is given firm indications of the type of information he is to look for. For example:

Worksheet 12

World War II: The Home Front

Imagine you are one of your family on a summer's day in 1940. Describe the day from when you get up until you go to bed. During the day there is an air raid. What happens? How do you, your friends and relatives feel about it? Points you may like to include are: sirens, shelters, gas-masks, blackout, the A.R.P., the A.F.S., fire-watching, guns, barrage-balloons and searchlights.

Some historians disparage such imaginative reconstructions as 'unhistorical' and accuse the teacher of handling the evidence too freely. In fact there is no more conflict between historical method and imaginative reconstruction than there is between the evidence of an archaeological site and an A. Sorrell reconstruction of it.[14] A heap of stones may say a great deal to the trained archaeologist, but even he may find difficulty in capturing the atmosphere of the building when it was in use. The reconstruction gives something to the expert and everything to the layman. The child writing his Family History within the limits imposed by the evidence is not merely using someone else's reconstruction: he is making his own. By recreating the past through the agency of the imagination, the child comes to terms with history at his own level of perception, transferring the raw material into an intellectually honest, personal interpretation of what happened.

At all stages of the project emphasis is laid on the use of the spoken and written language. The pupil will have to formulate and ask questions clearly and sustain a conversation. He will be given practice in letter-writing and keeping a diary, and he will have to arrange a considerable quantity of material into an acceptable literary form. Much of this, including the letter-writing, can be done in class. A letter written to elicit specific information from relatives will have a relevance which the conventional classroom letter, thanking an imaginary aunt for an imaginary present, can never have. A report giving the substance of an interview is worth any number of exercises in direct and indirect speech.

The child can also be introduced to quite sophisticated techniques such as filing originals or copies of correspondence and building up a class card-index of data. With older pupils, there could be abundant practice in shorthand, typing and office techniques and since these are being put to immediate, personal and practical use, there will be a strong motive for pupils to improve their performance.

Art and Drama

Children should be encouraged to express themselves not only through prose and poetry but also through art and drama. This may involve painting apprehensive evacuees in 1940 or an Edwardian street scene, or constructing a cardboard diorama of great-great grandparents' drawing room.

Plate 1. Great-great grandparents' drawing room.
Student's work, Berkshire College of Education

Children might even wish to paint or model in clay, or sculpt themselves or relatives. Similarly a teacher interested in drama can help groups of children relive Home-Front experiences during the

Second World War and other interesting episodes from the past of individual families.

Geography

The pupils should draw maps to illustrate the precise geographical contexts of their ancestors' homes, whether these were local or far away. They should also try to obtain pictures of the areas preferably from family or local collections, showing the districts as they were in their ancestors' lifetimes, or, if this is impossible, recently-taken photographs or picture postcards showing the areas as they are today. Older pupils or students can make detailed studies of the landforms, vegetation, climate, communications, industries and types of building to be found there.

The Immediate District

Especially in rural schools, but more often in towns and suburbs than one might suppose, the class will contain at least a few children whose families have lived in the district for several generations. These children can undertake a local study and investigate the role their ancestors played in the economy of the neighbourhood.

Neighbouring Areas

Many children's families will come from other parts of the county or from neighbouring counties. It should be possible for most of these pupils to make at least one or two visits with their parents to their places of origin, where they should be encouraged to talk to old people (not just their own relatives) and photograph, or obtain postcards, of interesting buildings and views. The teacher may find it helpful to devise a questionnaire listing the most important items he wishes the children to observe.

More distant areas

In a suburban school most of the class may come in this category. Roman Catholic schools in particular will contain many children whose families still maintain close links with relatives in Ireland. In all schools there are likely to be a few children of Irish origin, and also some from Scottish and Welsh families. Though in many cases the children's families will rarely, if ever, visit their ancestral area, this does not mean that children will be less interested in undertaking a project on it.

Family moves, visits and holidays

Another way of providing children with areas to study is to chart family moves and to plot the places where their relatives now live. This is particularly applicable where the children live on new housing estates.

More distant parts of the world can be studied by encouraging the children to contact relatives who have emigrated, and there is plenty of scope here for projects on sheep farming in Australia or life in Ontario. Similarly many of the children will have parents or grandparents who have had military service abroad. Whatever is done, the teacher should consider carefully whether to concentrate the attention of the whole class on one area, to divide it up into groups to study the areas associated with the families of two or three of the children in the class, or to allow the children to pursue their researches independently. The golden rule always is to ensure that resources are adequate for the particular mode of organisation selected.

Mathematics

The pooled information about families and the individuals who compose them can be used for all kinds of statistical and graph work. Younger children can find out the number of children in the family, and draw graphs of places of origin or of the popularity of leisure activities. Older pupils can draw general conclusions about the age at which successive generations left school, and establish demographic trends concerning the number of children in families and of age of marriage and death over several generations.

Genetics

With senior pupils, work on Family History provides an excellent introduction to the study of genetics, particularly if a biologist is available as a member of the team. Genetics is an important field of study not only because of the popular myths surrounding it, but also because the study of inherited characteristics noticeable even in a very short pedigree — especially if it includes numerous cousins — leads naturally to an examination of the laws of heredity.

All the children's families will exhibit some hereditary traits and pupils can attempt to work out the inheritance of easily observable characteristics such as the colour of eyes, left and right-handedness, hair colour, or attached and non-attached ear lobes. They can also study the distinction between inherited and acquired characteristics and consider particularly the common fallacious beliefs that inherited characteristics can blend, and that personality traits, such as a strong social conscience can be transmitted. This kind of work may also involve the consideration of misunderstandings about inbreeding and its effects, and the determination of sex by the male Y chromosome, while even superficial work on blood groups should be enough to destroy belief in popular myths about 'royal blood', 'blue blood' and 'blood relationships'. It may also lead to interesting work on the blood groups found in different races and a consideration of racial mixture.

Discussion of genetic data may lead senior pupils on to such questions as the relative importance of heredity and environment, illegitimacy, the population explosion and birth control, and the reputedly unusual intelligence of South African 'decompression babies'. Associated topics which might arise are artificial insemination and inovulation and the tampering with the structure of D.N.A. to produce human beings to order. These rather frightening possibilities are discussed at length in Gordon Rattray Taylor's *The Biological Time-Bomb* (1968). Clearly any such studies would involve discussion of whether the family in the form we know it has any long-term future.

Technology and Domestic Science

More technically minded pupils may become involved in studying the working of various types of industrial machinery, the agricultural tools or early motorised vehicles used by their ancestors. Some may wish to study improvements in domestic appliances and fittings; others may wish to try cooking to menus culled from wartime women's magazines or early editions of Mrs. Beaton. They might even try washing clothes without detergents! It would be mistaken to assume that only boys are likely to be interested in technical matters and only girls in 'home affairs'. In the authors' experience the reverse is almost as likely to be true.

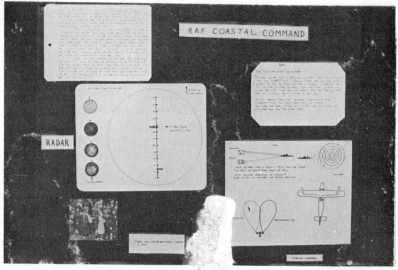

Plate 2. 12 Year old girl studies rad: den Erlegh School, Berkshire)

Photography

Elderly relatives are often prepared to lend photographs, but unwilling to see them incorporated in their grandchild's Family History file. Where there is a school photographic club, a copying service can be set up, thus greatly enhancing the children's Family Histories. An expert photographer can also help to date photographs by identifying the type of studio backdrop or photographic process employed (see below pp.89-92).

Beyond such 'servicing' lies much more creative work: making a film strip, *My Family History*, or even a short 8mm film. One could well argue that the medium of film has more imaginative possibilities for the recreation of the past than have writing, art, or drama. Through the clever use of film, old photographs can be brought to life. The immense possibilities of Family History material in the film medium have been well-illustrated by such television documentaries as John Gibson's *Tommy Steele in Search of Charlie Chaplin*, screened twice during 1971.

Economics

Although parents must not be questioned about their incomes, they will be only too eager to recall the cost of commodities in the past. One of the things the children can do is to make their own retail price index. Taking a basket of goods, they can trace back the cost of the articles over the past 50 years. Earnings can be deduced from advertisements in the local press and prices related to incomes. Pupils will inevitably meet evidence of great social changes. For instance, a cook of yesterday nearly always worked for a family; today she is more likely to be working in a school, factory or office kitchen.

Social Studies

In studying his own family, the child may come to appreciate the range of different jobs that people do and how they serve the community in different ways. Most primary schools undertake simple projects on occupations, and children often select those of their parents, friends or relatives. A postman's son may study the Post Office, an urban child who has a relative who is a farmer may want to find out exactly how a farm works. Interesting though such projects are, only too often they are carried out in a social vacuum. Yet the teacher can help the child at this stage to relate the occupation to the family unit (the father as wage-earner), and outwards to the community (the father as provider of a necessary service).

In most areas, a fair cross-section of occupations will be found not only amongst the parents of children in the class, but within individual families. In this way, the child may gradually come to realise how the family meshes with those institutions which serve him, like the school and the health service; with public utilities which provide light, heat and transport and with commercial bodies such as shops and banks, as well as institutions for spiritual and recreational needs, like the Church, theatres, cinemas, libraries, clubs and pubs. As this model of the family in its autonomous and more social roles becomes more complex, so the child is better able to think of his own family, not only in terms of its inter-actions and associations with local institutions, but also of how it fits into a wider regional or national context.

Thus, by investigating how families interact with each other and with institutions, both in the present and in the past, children may form clearer concepts of how society is composed, how it changes over a limited period, what the forces behind these changes are and how individuals and groups respond to change. An understanding of these relationships will also help the child to define his own rôle in society.

Notes and References

1   Schools' Council, *Humanities for the Young School Leaver – an approach through History* (1969), p.10.

2   Schools' Council, Working Paper No. 11, *Society and the Young School Leaver: a humanities programme in preparation for the raising of the school leaving age* (1967), pp. 39-40.

3   The Keele Integrated Studies Project, *A Handbook for Teachers*, draft version (1971), p.3.

4   L.A. Smith, 'Starting I.D.E.', in *Ideas*, no. 1 (1967), p.2.

5   Edward Mason, *Collaborative Learning* (1970), p.88.

6   M. Ballard, 'Change and the Curriculum', in *New Movements in The Study and Teaching of History* (1970), p.10.

7. *Ibid.*, p.10.

8   R. Wake, 'History as a Separate Discipline: The Case', in *Teaching History*, vol. 1, no. 3 (1970), p.

9   A. Marwick, *The Nature of History* (1970), p.242.

10 John Holt, *The Underachieving School*, Pelican edn. (1971), p.35.

11 Evelyn Waugh, *Officers and Gentlemen*, Penguin edn., p.222.

12 Charles Kingsley, *Alton Locke*.

13 J. Fines, *History* (Blond's Teacher's Handbook, 1969), p.viii.

14 See Alan Sorrell, *Living History* (1965).

3 A SOCIAL EXPERIENCE

> It is only in thought that the school and out of school world can
> be regarded as independent of each other . . . The two spheres
> form part of the same world and are so intimately connected with
> each other that any attempt to isolate them is futile.
>
> Sir John Adams, *Modern Developments
> in Educational Practice* (1928 edn.), p.26

PREOCCUPIED with destroying subject boundaries, interdisciplin-
arians have sometimes failed to see how much more a child's
enthusiasm and patterns of learning can be disrupted and stunted
by the iron curtains which all too often separate home and school,
school and community, work and recreation. Some teachers take
the view that 'just as we go to an ironmonger's for hardware, to a
fishmonger's for fish, to a bookseller for books, so we go to a school
for information. Schools are knowledge shops and teachers are
information-mongers. Their business consists in communicating a
certain amount of knowledge, and their duties are discharged as
soon as the agreed amount has been imparted'.[1] In demolishing
this insular view of the teacher's function, Adams stresses that
'in the last resort education consists in the manipulation of the
experience of the educand'.[2]

Peer-Group Activities

In manipulating this experience, it is likely that peer-group
activities will be ignored as of no importance. Yet in their famous
book, *The Lore and Language of Schoolchildren*, the Opies have
shown the richness and antiquity of the school-children's own
culture. There is no reason why this should not be brought from
the playground into the classroom. Family History is concerned
with the whole child in a total environment. It does not make
artificial distinctions between home, school and play, but encourages
a free flow of traffic between the different 'compartments' of a
child's life.

Teacher/Pupil Relationships

Once these barriers are broken down, the teacher's role must
inevitably be modified. In a Family History scheme, far from the
teacher's holding a monopoly in the transmission of knowledge,
the classroom becomes a place where experiences are shared, and
in which the teacher finds himself learning with his pupils.
Furthermore, if the scheme is to be a success, he must establish the
closest possible relationship with the children's parents.

Involving the Parents

The Plowden Report emphasizes that one of the essentials for educational advance is a closer partnership between the school and the parents: 'Home and Schools interact continuously . . . A strengthening of parental encouragement may produce better performance in school, and thus stimulate the parents to encourage more.' Thus Plowden recommends that parents should be encouraged to take the greatest possible interest in the work of the school, and should be frequent and welcome visitors.[3] This plea is re-iterated in a more recent publication of the Department of Education and Science.[4] Referring specifically to the problems of socially disadvantaged children, the Schools' Council comments that

> If teachers are to play a useful role in relating what is done at school to conditions at home, some way must be found of establishing relationships other than those which are made when something has gone wrong. It is hardly surprising that contacts with school are unwelcome to parents if they arise only in such circumstances.[5]

It stresses that 'for all pupils in all schools, reaching the parents is highly desirable: for disadvantaged pupils it is a crucial necessity'.[6] In practice, co-ordination between parents and teachers sometimes proves difficult. 'Some schools find that even films and slides do not bring parents close enough to children's learning.'[7] Furthermore, teachers are being urged to visit the parents at home. The Department comments:

> Many teachers visit homes occasionally; they may go when children are ill or to see the new baby; they may take children home when for some reason they are kept late at school. Others are ingenious in making opportunities to see fathers who do not turn up at the school. They may go 'to collect pigeons for a school talk, to see a collection of toy soldiers or to ask help for making things at the school.'[8]

At an early stage of any Family History project, the pupil will need to ask for parental help in supplying information and photographs, and when he moves on from his own autobiography to those of his parents, they are necessarily brought into the centre of the school work, and full parent-teacher co-operation may become a reality. This is a good point at which to call a meeting of parents to explain the remaining stages of the scheme and how they can help in it. It has been found that however carefully it is worded, a letter does not seem to be adequate. It seems to arouse immediate suspicions of prying. If it is not possible to call a meeting, it seems preferable to deal with any problems as they arise, if necessary visiting the homes of doubtful parents, rather than making any explanations by letter.

Teachers who have undertaken Family History projects have been surprised to see how some parents, who had previously taken

Plate 3 Involving the Parents (Stoneham School, Reading)

little interest in their children's school work, became involved in
it for the first time. Many parents helped with the research themselves. This bears out the claim in the Department of Education and
Science's survey that, 'Parents appreciate an opportunity to work
with teachers, understand more clearly the purpose of what is
being done and sympathize with the difficulties which are being
experienced'.[9] The survey recommends that the particular skills of
parents can be utilised in school:

> A father who is a commercial artist is preparing illustrations for a
> session on heraldry, and the local children's librarian has reviewed
> and discussed books with two nine-year olds in the head-
> master's fortnightly television magazine programme.[10]

While few would minimise the importance of this kind of
parental involvement, the fact remains that such parents are almost
invariably middle-class and already highly concerned about their
children's education. In a Family History project, all parents can be
equally involved, and the memories of a working-class parent who
left a slum school at 15 may be as vivid as those of a university
graduate. Nor do memories need to go very far back, for a child
on a modern housing estate to be introduced to a world very
different from his own. Few who watched the B.B.C. television
documentary *Tommy Steele and Things* on 21 December 1969,
could fail to enjoy the entertainer's nostalgic recreation of his own
boyhood weekly visit to the public baths, where, in a period of
three months, he would meet every mate he had ever known. Equally
compelling was his clandestine entry to the derelict Bermondsey

cinema, which was peopled once again in his imagination, and ours with the Saturday morning crowd of jostling unruly kids, re-enacting in the auditorium the battles on the screen. Most viewers who watched and enjoyed this programme would not realise that they were watching social history.

In some homes where family conversation is limited, Family History may possibly have a modest part to play in giving parents and children a focal point for conversation. For the first time, Dad may tell Johnny what it was like to be kids in Leyton during the Blitz. Dad never previously suspected Johnny would be interested; Johnny never thought of his father having anything interesting to tell.

Talking to Grandad

Although the involvement of parents is vital, the greater part of the information in a Family History project is likely to come from elderly relatives. Not only have they lived longer and therefore in most cases have more to tell, but they also have more leisure in which to tell it.

In conversations about the past, children and old people will find a new community of interest. By getting to know the person that Grandad once was, the child is likely to have more under-standing of Grandad as he now is. In this way, the child will be strengthening the family links which often act as a lifeline for elderly relatives. In his study of old people in Bethnal Green, Peter Townsend discovered that there the extended family was the norm, and the same must be true of many of the older districts of our towns and cities. Compared with family ties of 'blood, duty, affec-tion, common interest and daily acquaintance', he found that 'the ties of friendship, neighbourliness and club and church member-ship were neither so enduring nor so indissoluble'.[11] Townsend emphasizes that old people must be treated as an inseparable part of a family group. 'They are members of families and whether or not they are treated as such largely determines their security, their health and their happiness'.[12] Children can play their own modest part in keeping these family links strong.

There is an equal benefit for the child. In school, individual children are frequently submerged in the mass, particularly if they are neither very bright nor very dull, nor very conspicuous in the sporting or social life of the school. Such average children go through school with a minimum of individual attention. Almost as soon as they leave, their names are forgotten. For such children, the one-to-one relationship they can have in acquiring information from an elderly relative can be an important educational as well as social experience. For the first time in their school lives they are the focus of an adult's attention.

Children with Special Difficulties

Although most children's relatives will prove co-operative, nearly every class will contain at least one or two children who because of indifference on the part of their parents, or particular family difficulties, are unable to work on their own families. When Family History was introduced into Berkshire schools in 1968, the authors and the teachers were rather apprehensive about this problem and uncertain as to the best way of solving it, but in practice there were fewer difficulties than had been expected.

In all, out of over 700 children who have undertaken Family History projects, about 30 have posed special problems of one kind or another. In almost all cases, the difficulties have been circumvented satisfactorily. It is important that the child be engaged on a task which not only holds his interest, but can be seen by the other children to be directly relevant to the project as a whole, thus avoiding potentially embarrassing or hurtful comments. In one school a boy studied the teacher's family. More frequently the problem has been solved by the children with family difficulties either working on information acquired by their classmates or else collecting information themselves from local old people. (See below pp.35-36.)

Family Quarrels

The children's researches have sometimes reached an impasse because of a family quarrel which careful nurturing has kept evergreen — in fact few families are without the relative who is *persona non grata*. This position may well be justified on grounds of character, as the persistent child may eventually discover for himself, but more frequently it reflects a system of *apartheid* in the family. *Noveaux riches* do not always welcome visitors who draw the attention of their friends and neighbours to their humble origin. Obviously such a situation must be handled with tact, but few people, whatever their attitude to the child's family, will refuse to help the child.

Sometimes the family quarrels took place long enough ago for the immediate family not to be concerned about them, but even so they can prove a difficult obstacle. Here are two examples from children's work:

> When Florence died, the brothers split up the estate, but one brother, Alfred George, had quarrelled with the family and moved away. Since then no contact has been made with his brothers or their descendants and so there is great difficulty in tracing them.[13]

> As the story goes, my great-great-grandfather was a corn-miller and he lived near Birkenhead, Cheshire. He owned his own mill, married and had several children, one of which was my great-grandfather — Richard Clifford Bourn. When he had grown to a reasonable age he had a very intense quarrel with his father over some unknown matter. Each person's feelings on the subject were

so strong that the son, unable to tolerate life with his father, left
home, and then added an 'e' to the end of his name.[14]

There is no reason why children should be unduly shielded from
the fact that disagreements arise within any group of human beings,
and it is always valuable for the child to discover that there is more
than one side to an argument. The sensitive child will also gradually
become aware of his own family as a microcosm of society.

Family Skeletons

Sometimes, in talking to parents or relatives, the child will detect
a sudden drop in temperature and an abrupt change in the subject-
matter of the conversation. He has stumbled upon the scandal that
no-one talks about except in hushed whispers or after the children
have gone to bed. Where the teacher suspects that there might be
confidential family information which parents do not want either
school or child to know (e.g. Father served a prison sentence 10
years ago) he should direct the child's researches elsewhere. Skeletons
should be kept firmly locked away, and at all costs the teacher
must ensure that neither parents nor relatives imagine the school
wishes to pry into their private affairs. In practice we have found
that family skeletons, even when uncovered, seldom seem to
worry either the children concerned or their classmates. One 15-year-
old proudly volunteered the information in class discussion that,
'my Mum and Dad aren't married and my sister has a different Dad
who comes to see us sometimes'. This failed to arouse any noticeable response from his classmates. Members of another class were
extremely impressed when one of the children revealed that his
mother claimed to be the illegitimate offspring of a country girl
who had been led astray by the local landlord, a member of a
family whose name is a household word.

This illustrates a further point. In a surprising number of cases
the parents showed as little reticence as the children and were
willing to give uncensored details. For example, one 14-year-old
wrote of an aunt:

> She married Richard Fish in 1940. They had one child . . . The
> marriage was dissolved in 1947, and she married William
> Templeton. They had two children . . . The second marriage was
> dissolved in 1962 and she married Wallace Gibbs in 1968.[15]

In a few cases, however, parents refused to co-operate and gave
no reason. Here one may suspect that there were personal factors
involved, of which the teacher was unaware, e.g. divorce, or
parental illegitimacy. Naturally, in such cases the parents' privacy
was protected.

Adopted and Fostered Children

It was found that these children normally had little difficulty in drawing up family trees, as they could work on those of their adoptive parents or guardians.

Immigrants

Teachers whose classes contain a fair proportion of first and second generation immigrants need not assume that a Family History project is inappropriate for their particular school. Of course, it is true there will be various special problems. For instance, it is often very difficult to contact kinsfolk, and even if their whereabouts are known, there may be a language barrier, or the relatives may be illiterate. Inevitably, there will be long delays in correspondence. Some immigrant parents may be suspicious of the teacher's motives. Often, family documents will be very sparse. On the other hand, such children may have more to offer to the project than others in the class, in that they are representatives of countries and cultures very different from our own. The children can collect information from magazine articles, newspapers, television reports and handouts from Embassy information services. Better still, it is sometimes possible for the relatives of the children to come into the school to talk to the class, or to contact a school in their home country in order to arrange an exchange of photographs and information.

In *Parents are Welcome*, McGeeney stresses how the response of Asian parents is 'conditioned by the attitudes of an extended family. These kinship consultations extend to their village of origin'. Referring to the experience of Spring Grove Primary School, Huddersfield, which has developed a special reception centre for immigrant children from five to 15 he comments:

> It is heartening for Mr. Burgin and his colleagues to know from letters which are read to them that families in Jullunder and Lyallpur, long before they come to this country, are aware that there is in Huddersfield a truly multiracial school, which gives no preference to any children on grounds of race, colour or creed.[16]

The involvement of immigrant families in a Family History project will make it clear to English children that whilst language, climate, temperament, colour and creed may be very different, foreigners are people — many live in families very like their own, enjoy the same things such as football and television, and often have the same ambitions. This interchange of information may prove as important for the teacher as for the children. The Department of Education and Science has stressed that 'English teachers . . . often need more information about the background and conventions of immigrants'.[17] It is important that the immigrant child should be given the feeling that the teacher has almost as much to learn from him as he has from the teacher.

A surprisingly large number of children's families originate from Poland, Cyprus, Italy, Malta and other European countries.

In the Family History projects undertaken to date, two of the most exciting were done by children of Jugoslav and Polish origin.

Co-operative Work

In every class there are one or two children who can obtain a lot of information about the past way of life on their parents or grandparents — far more than they themselves can use. This information can be pooled, thereby not only solving a practical difficulty, but implementing a sound educational principle: children should be encouraged to help each other.

Teachers using a Family History scheme should always try to devise methods in which all the general information on social history may be pooled.

Help from the Old

Grandad Goes Back to School

One way of solving the problem of children with special difficulties is to invite old people to visit the school and talk to the children. Not only does this create a 'living history lab' in the school

Plate 4. Grandad goes back to School (Maiden Erlegh School)

but in many cases it gives local old people a high spot in their week — particularly when tea and transport are provided. Invariably the children are eager questioners and ready listeners.

Many aspects of a Family History scheme can be applied directly to work with local old people rather than with relatives. In order to give children unable to work on their own families a task which is equally demanding and stimulating, they can be asked to produce an edited tape recording (perhaps in the form of a radio programme)

Plate 5. 'Eager questioners and ready listeners' (Maiden Erlegh School)

of an old person's life story. This can take many hours of hard work, but most children enjoy it and take pride in gaining technical mastery of the equipment. If tackled as a full-scale project, with oral memories complemented by research into local social history and illustrated by slides, the project can be just as absorbing as Family History and can make a major contribution to the overall scheme.

Visiting Local Old People

Children without elderly relatives living nearby can be encouraged to visit and talk to local old people. Many of these are very lonely, and welcome the children's visits. In many cases these lead to the children's offering to undertake jobs such as shopping, weeding the garden or decorating. Of course, such work is already undertaken in a great many schools, usually as part of 'community service', but its development out of a Family History project has two distinct advantages. First, the old person is approached because he or she can help the child and not *vice-versa*. Many elderly people are too proud to accept help readily, but are only too delighted to give it. Then, after several visits, information can be exchanged for assistance in house or garden: the traffic is two-way. Second, the child is seeing not just an anonymous 'old person' in need of help, but someone whom he may get to know well through reaching a sympathetic understanding of a bygone age. Old people living today have experienced a telescoping of time; the world has not merely changed, it has become transformed. What old people miss most are the deceased relatives and friends who shared their memories of the world they have lost. No-one can ever completely fill this gap, but sensitivity towards the old person's past can go a long way

towards bridging it. The gratitude of some old people for small
kindnesses can be almost embarrassing. 'May you . . . be greatly
blessed for your help in bringing them up to think of the aged',
wrote one old lady to a Headmaster.[18] If children can be given a
real involvement in the past, they can scarcely fail to feel a kinship
with those who were themselves young many years ago. Without a
feeling for the past, however kind they may be, children are unlikely
to see old people as anything but coelacanths, for whom there is
no real place in the last quarter of the 20th century.

It is interesting to note that in the Schools' Council Working
Paper 17, *Community Service and the Curriculum* (HMSO, 1968)
despite many excellent suggestions of ways in which children can
help old people, there is scarcely a mention of the mutual benefits
of carrying on an extended conversation with them. Indeed a child
who came to dig the garden but was prevented from doing so by a
heavy conversational barrage, and went back to school leaving the
sod unturned would probably feel frustration and guilt at the way
his time had been 'wasted'.

Community service in schools should raise its sights above
digging gardens, decorating and going shopping, important though
this material help is. It should also provide old people with someone who can alleviate their loneliness by listening to their memories,
and who can share vicariously in their past. The mental well-being
of the old is even more important than the physical. Loneliness
does not consist in living alone. An old person living with relatives
who show no interest in the past may be more lonely than one
living alone but visited regularly by a contemporary.[19]

Just as important as the young's coming to appreciate the
problems of the old, is giving the old an insight into the younger
generation's modes of thought. The old lady who is very apprehensive of opening her door to a scruffy, long-haired youth in
patched jeans and T-shirt may find, on further acquaintance, that,
beneath the unprepossessing exterior lies an idealism and social
concern that was rare among the youth of her own generation.

The problem of communication between young and old is a
growing one. By 1980, 16% of the population will be over 60.
Society should be giving careful thought to how to educate both
young and old to build a community which is based on something
more than peaceful co-existence.

Family History embraces both past and present. It asks what
values are universal and which are determined by time and place.
In so doing it generates a dialogue which can help to bridge the
generation gap by means of a sympathetic understanding of
different points of view.

Notes and References

1 Sir John Adams, *Modern Developments in Educational Practice* edn. (1928), p.27. For a recent American indictment of the system *see* J. Holt, *The Underachieving School*, Pelican edn. (1971), pp.22-36.

2 Adams, *op. cit.*, pp.28-29.

3 Department of Education and Science, *Children and Their Primary Schools: A Report of the Central Advisory Council for Education England*, vol. 1, (1967), pp.37-49. *See also* J.W.B. Douglas, *The Home and the School* (1964), Chap. VII.

4 Department of Education and Science, *Parent/Teacher Relations in the Primary School, Education Survey 5*. (1968), p.22.

5 Schools' Council, *Working Paper 27, Cross'd with Adversity* (1970) p.101.

6 *Ibid.*, p.98.

7 Department of Education and Science, *op. cit.*, p.21.

8 *Ibid.*, p.19. *See also* Schools' Council, *op. cit.*, p.96-97; P. McGeeney, *Parents are Welcome* (1969), pp.109-112.

9 Department of Education and Science, *op. cit.*, p.26.

10 *Ibid.*, p.27.

11 Peter Townsend, *The Family Life of Old People*, abridged, Penguin ed. (1963), p.229.

12 *Ibid.*, p.227.

13 14-year-old boy's account. The names have been changed and places omitted.

14 Another 14-year-old boy. Names have been changed. Although family tradition attributes the variant spelling to the quarrel, this is most unlikely to be its cause, for surname spellings were still fluid in the 19th century. *See below* pp.136-7.

15 Stoneham School, Reading. Names and dates have been changed.

16 Patrick McGeeney, *op. cit.*, p.122.

17 Department of Education and Science, *op. cit.*, p.33.

18 Stoneham School, Reading.

19 Two useful films on the loneliness of old age are *Application* (10 mins., Royal Netherlands Embassy, 1965), and *I think they call him John* (John Krish, distributed by Contemporary Films, 1964). The Church of Scotland A.V.A. Distribution Centre have produced *Only Lonely*, a 10 mins., 3¾ ips tape.

4 A DISCIPLINED FREEDOM

> Before attempting to introduce the children to a new type of problem, the teacher must scrutinize the concepts involved, attempt to analyse them and isolate the essential components. The components are then presented in a graded sequence so that the pupil can see these basic units clearly and work with them. The teacher should also make clear to the pupil the way in which the sub-units of the problem are interconnected.
>
> E. Stones, *An Introduction to Educational Psychology* (1966), p.371.

MOST EDUCATIONALISTS are agreed that at the root of all worthwhile learning lies motivation. However enlightened the project, unless the children's enthusiasm has been aroused it is of little value:

> The teacher is no nearer making the pupils active participants in what they learn by simply imposing on them an activity unrelated to their readiness to become active, than he is by merely talking to them.[1]

Freedom of Choice

That one of the most crucial factors in motivation is freedom of choice has been generally accepted since the principle was almost forced upon a sceptical profession by the pioneers of child-centred learning — Maria Montessori, John Dewey, A.S. Neill, and a host of lesser lights in the educational pantheon. This freedom was the *raison d'etre* of the Dalton Plan of the 1920s. Since the Second World War, it has been one of the principal factors in the revolution in Primary Schools, and in the last decade its impact has begun to be felt in Secondary and Higher Education. Freedom of choice is, however, more than a device to maintain interest in the subject. It has much broader educational implications:

> A teacher may help and guide, but he must not arrogantly choose what his pupil is to do; interests are many and various, and not always easily perceptible to a busy teacher. Education in making sound choices is most important in an age where the preservation of individuality and provision for the wise use of leisure time are the two most vital parts of personal development.[2]

The emphasis on the liberty of the individual child to learn what interests him has caused the widespread adoption of the *topic* or *project* approach in Primary Schools. In Secondary Schools, progress has been much slower, although the Schools' Council takes the view that 'Topics have helped to contribute to the secondary school something of the enthusiasm that this sort of activity engenders in the primary school'.[3]

Peter Rance sees the five characteristics of topic work as: placing the main emphasis on the child rather than on the subject, encouraging him 'to construct his own method of approach to knowledge', the provision of opportunities to 'learn how to learn', the breaking down of subject barriers even though the starting point for the main theme may be provided by an academic subject, and the necessity of allowing a child to acquire knowledge through his natural curiosity about his environment.[4]

Some educationalists carry freedom of choice much further. As we have seen, in the Interdisciplinary Enquiry component of the Fourfold Curriculum developed at Goldsmiths' College, the teacher becomes a consultant who provides suggestions, books and references, thus shifting the onus of learning to the pupils. (See above, p. 15).

Expectations Unfulfilled

However, the adoption in many schools of a child-centred approach to learning has often failed to achieve the success that was eagerly anticipated. Instead of being spoonfed by the teacher, the child, cut off from the communal supply of nourishment, is left to forage for himself. Either he is unable to digest the over-rich diet offered him, or else he fails to find enough food to keep alive. Thus, because of vagueness of aims and deficiencies in structure and resources, the child's performance is often pitiful. He is considerably worse off than he would have been if he had been taught in a fairly traditional manner by a stimulating teacher. It is even doubtful if his new learning situation offers a better bill-of-fare than he might have received from the dullest of class teachers. Mindless copying from inappropriate books is as excruciatingly boring and as soul-destroying as copying the teacher's notes from the blackboard. Adding a few drawings may make the task more congenial, and even, marginally, more educative; but it is a mistake to call even the best of the resulting scrapbooks and magazines, all neatly labelled — a well-executed drawn sketches of Victorian furniture based on illustrations in books and magazines, all neatly labelled — a well executed masterpiece of the copyist's craft. This is no more history than is collecting cigarette-cards depicting historical costumes, motor-cars or soldiers' uniforms. This is not to deny the place of drawings in a project. They have their place, but it is secondary to the main purpose of learning history. History is about people. It involves learning about how people lived in periods other than our own. It is not the ottoman in which the historian is interested but its designer and the people who reclined upon it. Why was this piece of furniture designed in this particular way? What sort of society demanded such articles? Who in Victorian society could afford to buy them? The artefact is used to provoke the questions *How?* and *Why?*.

Part of the pleasure of teaching history is in stimulating children and students to ask such important questions. Yet many children find it even more difficult to ask the right questions than to find answers to them. Prosser notes that both the new American science curricula[5] and the English Nuffield 'O' Level courses seem to have been successful and stimulating with clever children, but much less so with average and less able children. Clearly a great many of these children lack the maturity, experience and skill necessary to implement the second of Rance's criteria by constructing their 'own method of approach to knowledge'. Prosser comments ruefully that 'We seem to have developed a large number of innovations all at once on a largely *ad hoc* basis, and many of them have been proliferated by fashion rather than from any rational background. Considerations of structuring affect them all, yet one fails to find any detailed justification in these terms for most of them'. He asks what degrees of freedom we can allow in discovery and topic approaches, and stresses the need to develop a coherent structure for unstreamed classes and for individual learning programmes.[6]

A Structured Freedom

With the rival claims of freedom and structure equally strident and equally strong, it seems clear that less able children will take an interest in a project, ask themselves the right questions, and produce worthwhile answers only if the project is highly structured, but at the same time is felt by the pupils to be relevant and meaningful, and allows maximum personal choice within the structure. This has been particularly stressed in the United States. Thus Woodruff emphasizes that 'structure does not imply autocratic teacher domination of the lesson, but rather the overall pattern in which students will pursue their learning activities'. He notes that individual sessions 'make their best contribution to student progress when each one presents one significant concept or skill from a well planned sequence of concepts and skills, and when each lesson is planned so that it follows the natural processes of teaching and learning'.[7] Lee makes a strong case out for joint teacher-pupil planning which he defines as the 'co-operative selection of subject-matter, content and methods of pedagogical attack'. This, he says, 'could do much to integrate pupil needs and interests into the structuring of the learning situation'.[8]

Outline of a Family History Scheme

Family History is ideally suited to this kind of joint teacher-pupil planning. However, there must inevitably be many different kinds of Family History project. Although they may all share a common core, every teacher needs to devise a structure to suit his own aims and the needs of his pupils. For this reason, the Family History Scheme which the authors have been developing over the past four years consists of two elements: the *Main Line Programme*, which can be adapted to suit the needs of children of any age and ability; and *Branching Programmes*, designed to show what part Family History can play in fulfilling the various historical, interdisciplinary or social objectives and preferences of teachers, while continuing to meet the various needs of pupils of different ages and abilities. A series of detailed guides for teachers consisting of a Main-line programme book and a number of Branching Programme books is in an advanced stage of preparation. Here is a provisional summary of their contents.

The Main Line Programme

This is a sociological and historical study of five generations. It consists of three phases divided into 20 units.[9] Each phase has limited and clearly defined objectives. Historical concepts are developed from the kind of work with which primary school children are already familiar, particularly in English and mathematics. Only slowly and cautiously is an historical element introduced. It is not until the second phase that the programme becomes predominantly historical, and even then the history is not, perhaps, of a kind many teachers would recognise. It is assumed that by the time the child begins to work on the third phase he will have a rudimentary understanding of the basic historical concepts such as *time, change, continuity* and *evidence*, and be able to develop them by working on much more difficult material. (It is not, of course, envisaged that any teacher will plough relentlessly through all 20 units!)

The Main Line Programme also provides an opportunity for the child to work in three different situations: as an individual, as a member of a group and as a member of the class. It is important that

1. the classroom organisation allow adequate time for individual consultations;

2. thought be given to the formation of groups based on friendships and a spread of ability;[10]

3. time be found for formal sessions where a common core of background information is provided, and in which the individual and group topics are co-ordinated through class discussion, drama or an exhibition.

An overall picture of the whole programme will be found inside the back cover. Here is a more detailed breakdown of the content of the various units.

Phase I WHO AM I? *(Generation I, c.1960 - Date)*
Units 1 - 5

The child's own autobiography is used to introduce him to a meaningful concept of *time* through an understanding that he himself has a past (Unit 2) and time is expressed visually on his personal *Retrograph* (Unit 1), a chart on which the lives of child, parents, grandparents and more remote ancestors are visibly correlated

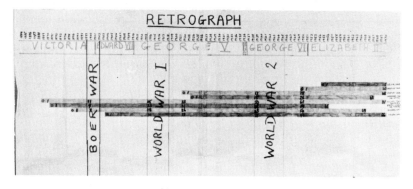

Plate 6. A Retrograph

with events. His nine or 12 years are used as a manageable unit, longer than the year, but much shorter than the traditional century. He is helped to realise that he himself is part of the continuum of past, present and future. He is also introduced to the concept of *evidence* through the oral, archaeological,[11] pictorial and documentary sources which he uses to write his own life-story (Unit 2). He is made aware of the need to conserve different forms of historical evidence surviving from the past, and to play his part in ensuring that evidence of our own age is left for posterity. Through the *Classroom Museum* (Units 2, 3 and 4), he is given experience of the need for the accurate identification of evidence, and of how objects may be classified according to certain shared characteristics. This stage also seeks to give the child an objective view of his own way of life and an insight into important changes that have taken place in his lifetime (Unit 3) or may occur in the future (Unit 4). General conclusions are drawn from pooled data (Units 1, 4). Thus the child is introduced to the concept of generalisation made on the basis of evidence, and is given a yardstick by which to compare the childhoods of other generations studied later in the programme.

Apart from fulfilling these major objectives, the *Who Am I?* project can also play a part in the development of literary, mathematical, recording and artistic skills and can be used by the teacher as a launching platform for all kinds of interdisciplinary work.

Plate 7. *Who Am I?* in progress,
Meadowvale County Primary School, Bracknell, Berks.

Although seven and eight year olds are capable of tackling the
Who Am I? project (see p. 155) the full Family History scheme may
prove too difficult for them. It is probably best started at the upper
end of the Primary School or in the junior forms of the Secondary.
Although many of the suggestions it contains are applicable to
younger children and some to older pupils, it has been devised with
the age group of nine to 13 in mind. Obviously, with older
secondary pupils the work in this stage of the scheme can be
telescoped, but even they should begin with a study of themselves
and the society to which they belong.

Phase 2 INVOLVING THE PARENTS
(Generation 2, c.1935 - Date)
Units 6 - 10

In the course of Phase 2 the child writes simple biographies of his
two parents, thus extending his ideas of *time, continuity* and
change to cover a manageable, but none-the-less momentous,
period of social and technological innovation. He also draws up a
basic family tree. Particular emphasis is laid upon the childhood
of his parents and upon their experiences on the Home Front
during the Second World War, the information being obtained
through a series of questionnaires on topics such as meals, family
relationships, shopping or evacuation.

Phase 3 THE HISTORIAN AT WORK
(Generation 3, 1918-1945; Generation 4, 1890-1930;
Generation 5, 1865-1900)
Units 11 - 20

The child now really gets to grips with history. First he obtains information from his elderly relatives (unit 11). This is critically examined (unit 12), and amplified from the study of primary and secondary sources (unit 13). This threefold process is repeated for Generations 4 (units 14, 15, 16), and 5 (units 17, 18, 19). Thus the *Historian at Work* phase seeks to give the children a rich historical experience both by giving them a basic training in the ways an historian acquires and uses evidence, and by helping them to recreate the very different world in which their ancestors lived.

Overlapping generations

Obviously generations overlap; sometimes as many as four generations in a family may be living at the same time, but for practical reasons each generation has here been set in a specific historical period which will be studied intensively. An overlap of about 10 years has been allowed for each period in order to give the Family History continuity; otherwise the child might see it as a series of disconnected studies. In the case of such overlaps, the material is allocated to one generation of the other on practical grounds. For example, The Home Front of the Second World War is dealt with in Stage 2 because it is likely to figure prominently in parents' childhood memories, whereas increasingly the parents of today's children had little personal experience of actual combat. Other aspects of the Second World War are therefore, reserved for Phase 3. Similarly, it is likely to have been Great-grandfather (Generation 4) rather than Grandfather (Generation 3), who was actively involved in the General Strike, although Grandfather may well remember the hardships of the 1920s. Thus the child explores the past by a series of retrospective studies, bound together by his personal retrograph.

Evaluation

It is important that evaluation procedures should be built into any scheme of work, otherwise they tend to be overlooked. The last unit in each phase, therefore, is devoted to simple procedures aimed at testing whether the children have made progress in their grasp of historical concepts and skills.

The Historian at Work

Let us now consider in more detail the structure of the three stages of the *Historian at Work*.

Talking to Grandad

Information is obtained from elderly relatives in three stages — *genealogical, biographical* and *historical.* First, comprehensive family trees are built up; then the children find out more about the people on them; finally they ask questions about the world in which those people lived. For Generation 4 there may be few, if any, living relatives and the child may have to depend on hearsay evidence recounted by grandparents and information obtained from local old people or the relatives of other children in the class. Although for Generation 5 all the evidence will take the form of oral tradition, a lot of information can be obtained, as the examples quoted in Chapter 5 show.

Evaluating the Evidence (Units 12, 15 and 18)

In these units, historical concepts and techniques are introduced in progressive order of difficulty, using the raw material obtained in *Talking to Grandad.* Unit 12 (*Is It True?*) examines the validity of oral evidence (12.1), considers various kinds of bias (12.2), and using fairly concrete examples, introduces the pupil to simple comparisons between the generations (12.3). Unit 15 is devoted to quantification in history. The available evidence is reduced to statistics and conclusions are drawn from it, leading pupils to consider the complex question of causation in history. Unit 18 revises and develops the work of Units 12 and 15 using more difficult material. The work on the validity of first-hand oral evidence done in the course of Unit 12 is here continued with reference to oral tradition. In the comparisons now made between the five generations, particular consideration is given to the more abstract questions of relationships and attitudes within the home. This work leads naturally first to a consideration of changes in social attitudes generally and then to a discussion of the contradictory beliefs in 'progress' and in a past 'Golden Age'.

Painting the Backcloth (Units 13, 16 and 19)

In each stage, the oral evidence is verified and supplemented from secondary sources, so that individual biographies are set against the background of the social fabric and major historical events of the time. However, just as the main aim of the *Evaluating the Evidence* units is to develop the pupils' critical abilities, so the primary aim of the *Painting the Backcloth* units is to give the children rich imaginative experiences. This may be achieved by means of assignments which require the children to put themselves in their ancestors' shoes, e.g. Great-grandfather in the Trenches, Grannie preparing a meal in the 1930s on housekeeping money from the dole, Dad evacuated at seven years old. The experiences on which the child bases his imaginative reconstructions may be drawn from any aspect of life in any of the generations so long as the emphasis is placed on the way people lived, felt and thought.

Problems of Selection

Because of the wealth of potential 'backcloth' material, if he is to maintain a balanced Family History programme, a child will be able to study only a few themes in the life of any generation. Three methods of selection are possible:

1.   The choice of the same themes in the study of every generation ('Line of development'). This emphasises change and continuity, but carries with it the danger that the themes may become divorced from the rest of the social fabric. Apart from implying that change arises by some evolutionary process rather than as a result of contemporary pressures, a 'line of development' scheme also results in a lack of variety. If a child is not interested in say *transport*, he cannot take refuge in studying something else.

2.   The choice of different themes for each generation continually provides fresh centres of interest, but gives no basis for assessing continuity and change and the project loses its coherence.

3.   The best solution is to offer a mixture of *focal* and *optional* studies. In the course of pursuing the focal studies the child will observe the operation of continuity and change over five generations. The optional studies will help him to build up an overall impression of a single generation by considering various other aspects of its social life.

Focal Studies

The themes inseparable from any meaningful concepts of the family and the individual are *The Home* and **Clothes**. A family without a home ceases to be a family and becomes a social casualty, and an individual's clothes usually express his personality and social pretensions. To these themes we would add *School*, as the other institution most relevant to the child, and (in the third phase) *Religion*, the mainspring of all forms of social life for earlier generations.

The Home

There is more to a home than bricks and mortar, interior decoration and furniture. Every bit as important as these are the relationships within the house, between husband and wife, parents and children and, in Generations 4 and 5 perhaps employer and servant. To many this may seem a truism, but a cursory glance at many school projects (and published topic books) on *Homes* will confirm that a statement of the obvious is needed. To emphasise the human element, the enquiries on this topic have therefore been given titles such as *Grandparents at Home*.

Clothes

How few projects in school are actually undertaken on clothes! Though a topic variously entitled *Costume, Dress* or *Fashion* is always one of the most popular with girls, this rarely concerns itself with the clothes which Great-grandfather wore. In such studies not only is there frequently a strong bias towards ladies' fashions, but there is also a very undemocratic preoccupation with clothes worn by only a tiny fraction of the population. Girls draw pictures of crinolines and bustles – perhaps even of top hats and fancy waistcoats – but they seldom have the remotest idea about the clothes their great-grandparents wore at home, at work and at church. Rarely do they think of looking at Grannie's photograph album to find out.

School

Most children enjoy comparing the education (or lack of it) received by successive generations. Sometimes the contrasts can be striking. For example, the grandfather of one of the authors started work at eight years old, scaring crows and picking up stones, after a total education of only six months at the village school. His daughter achieved that pinnacle of working class aspirations – training as a teacher – and the author himself had a university education. Younger children will find most interest, perhaps, in changes in classrooms, content, method and discipline.

Religion

In earlier generations, for rural communities the church or chapel was the most important social institution outside the home, and it retained its hold over many rural communities until after the Second World War, playing an important part in moulding both home and school life. Even in suburban and some urban areas it remained the hub of middle-class social activities between the Wars. Quite young children can gradually come to appreciate the part that religion played in their ancestors' lives; However, both because of the relatively abstract nature of the subject and because parents are sensitive about the treatment of it, it is better not to introduce any reference to religion at the *Who Am I?* stage of the programme. The relative 'godlessness' of the present age will become apparent to children later, when they make comparisons between generations.

Optional Studies

These may be of three kinds. First, the child will need information relevant only to his own ancestors, e.g., if Great-grandfather was a blacksmith at Yeovil in Somerset, it should not be very difficult for the pupil to discover something about both blacksmiths and Yeovil. Secondly, the child can study some more general topic, such as *food* or *transport*. Here, he should be given complete freedom of choice. Thirdly, more senior pupils may wish to concentrate upon a particular event or movement, such as the *General Strike* or the *Suffragettes*. Those of Irish or foreign extraction may wish to choose events such as the Easter Rising of 1916 or the Nazi Invasion of Poland.

Losing Great-grandfather

Although most children soon become involved in optional studies, there is a danger that an ancestor may become the centre of a vast and tangled web of unfamiliar material. At almost every point in the study, the child will be faced with an enormous number of possible choices and he may lose sight of his ancestor altogether as one topic leads him on to another. There are three principal ways in which the pupil may 'lose' Great-grandfather.

1. He may seek to do the impossible and attempt to write a comprehensive history of the last 100 years, with a great deal of geographical and other material thrown in for good measure. Instead, he should be helped to look at familiar aspects of his own or his ancestors' environment in an historical way, or to reconstruct specific events with which his ancestors were associated.

2. Choosing an option such as *Railways*, the pupil may, as has been mentioned already in criticism of many such projects, confine himself to drawing pictures of locomotives. While illustration should be encouraged, it should be related to specific changes that the child has discovered. It is the effect of such changes on people's lives that is really important.

3. The pupil may flit from one unrelated piece of information to another. He may use the fact that Grandfather was once a platelayer on the Great Western to interpolate hefty chunks of the story of the railway into his history, or, even worse, write a potted history of the railways from Stephenson's Rocket to diesel expresses. Fascinating though such branch lines are, they are irrelevant to a Family History Main Line Programme. At this stage, the child's concern should be to record those facts which his grandfather remembers, such as picketing the local goods-yard during the General Strike, or the difficulty of raising a family on low wages prior to 1939.

Work-cards

As yet there is no strong tradition of work cards or worksheets in the secondary school, but where large numbers of children are simultaneously engaged on individual projects, they are almost essential if the pupils are to make any serious and systematic attempt to evaluate and augment the oral evidence they have collected. Questions should be of fairly general application.

Branching Programmes

Some of the Branching Programmes follow the completion of the Main-Line Programme. Others are designed to be integrated into it. One may move from Family History into more general historical work or beyond the frontiers of history teaching altogether.

About Myself (7-10)

This short two-unit programme is designed to prepare younger children for the Main-Line Programme. Children look at themselves, their way of life and the various social groups to which they belong.

Teaching Time Concepts (5-15 plus)

Here a Family History project is used in conjunction with a more lengthy programme designed to cope with the difficulties of teaching time concepts. The programme is an interdisciplinary one, starting in the Infants' School, and dealing systematically with the mathematical and scientific as well as the historical aspects of *time*.

A Changing World

Unit 3 of the Main-Line Programme deals with change and continuity in the focal elements *Home, Clothes* and *School* during the child's own lifetime. This branching programme offers work-cards on various options: *The Environment, Shopping, The Railways, Roads, The Sea, Air Transport,* and *Space Exploration*.

The Patch (8-16)

The Main-Line Programme is here combined with a Patch study of a particular period, such as the Edwardian Age or the Second World War, which is introduced into the study of the appropriate generation in order to place it in a broader perspective. Stress is laid on group work and study through activity methods.

The Topic (14-16)

The term *topic* is used here both for the type of 3-5,000 word Personal Topic undertaken for C.S.E. and for the group topic in which a single subject such as *The Edwardian Home*, or *The North African Campaign*, is studied in depth, either in conjunction with a Main-Line Programme, or with a Patch study.

Crossing the Frontiers (14-16)

Family History here is used as the central study from which to branch out into other subjects, particularly social studies and genetics. This programme is designed to meet the needs of school leavers and Sixth formers taking General Studies courses.

Further Back (14 plus)

Older children who are particularly interested can be encouraged to trace their ancestors further back, supplementing standard genealogical techniques with studies in the background social, economic, political and religious history.

Looking for Local History (9 plus)
The Main-Line Programme is integrated with a Neighbourhood study, which can be followed either by a Village or Urban Study based on a local family of gentry or businessmen, or by demographic work.

The Dynasts (11 plus)
Once the children have studied the last century or so through their own families, the teacher may wish to use the same principle for the study of another period of history (e.g. the 16th century) by viewing it through the eyes of a family prominent in national or local affairs, such as the Percys or Talbots.

The Apprentice Historian (16 plus)
Older pupils and students can engage in a more sophisticated evaluation of the reliance that can be placed upon oral and other forms of historical evidence and on the generalisations in secondary sources.

Welsh, Irish and Scottish Ancestors
Reasons are advanced for the major migrations, and help given with nomenclature, sources and 'backcloth' material.

Family History for Immigrants
A parallel programme is devised to meet the particular needs and difficulties of first, second and third generation immigrants, with separate sections concerned with West Indians, Asians, Jews and other European immigrants.

Although the branching programmes differ very considerably in subject matter, all but the *Apprentice Historian* (designed for sixth-formers or students) share one feature in common: they are, like the Main-Line programme, child-centred rather than subject-centred. The 'topic' or 'project' approach is implicit throughout. Some Secondary teachers are suspicious of such child-centred work because it makes it difficult to assess the child's day-to-day progress — a comparatively easy matter if one uses conventional classroom exercises. They also feel that child-centred work is difficult to examine. Our present methods of assessment may in fact be too blunt to measure such things as research initiative, creativity in presentation, oral contribution, individual fulfilment. More subtle still, we have hardly yet begun to consider the role of the individual in a group: his organisational ability, his contribution to re-inforcing the group's purpose and his critical attitude towards its output. To date, most learning in Secondary Schools has been based upon competition; nobody has yet shown that this is any more efficient than co-operation.

Notes and References

1   C.F. Strong, *History in the Secondary School* (1958), pp.87-88.

2   J. Fines and D.J. Steel, 'College of Education Students in the Archives Office', in *Archives* vol. 9, no. 41 (April 1969), p.24. *See also* Herbert R. Kohl, *The Open Classroom* (1970), p.56.

3   The Schools' Council, *The Certificate of Secondary Education: The Place of the Personal Topic – History*. Examinations Bulletin No.18 (1968), para. 81, p.21.

4   P. Rance, *Teaching by Topics* (1968), p.10.

5   These arose out of a series of conferences convened by J.S. Bruner in the late 1950s and early 1960s. The Working Conference on Research on Children's Learning (supported by the U.S. Office of Education through the Co-operative Research Program) held at Cambridge, Mass., June 1963, is reported in full in J.S. Bruner (ed.), *Learning about Learning: A Conference Report*, Washington (1966).

6   P. Prosser, 'Structuring in Curriculum Reform', *The New Era*, Vol. 52 (April 1971), p.487.

7   Asahel D. Woodruff, *Basic Concepts of Teaching* (San Francisco 1961), p.173.

8   James M. Lee, *Principles and Methods of Secondary Education* (New York, 1963), p.272.

9   Certain features of the scheme resemble those of American unit plans, where a programme is built from a combination of *resource units* and *teaching units*, the former laying down general principles and methods for enriching the latter. American resource units include such items as extensive bibliographies, suggested problem areas, methods of analysing pupil needs, suggestions for evaluating various educational outcomes. The teaching units contain specific exercises which can be implemented immediately in the classroom. *See* Lee, *Principles and Methods of Secondary Education*, New York (1963), pp.201-208; 271: Roland C. Faunce and Nelson L. Bossing, *Developing the Core Curriculum*, 2nd edn., New York (1958): Grace S. Wright, *Core Curriculum Development: Problems and Practices*, Bulletin No. 5, Washington (1955): Harold Alberty, *Re-organizing the High School Curriculum*, New York (1953), pp.169-191.
    Although the pattern of the authors' scheme is very similar to the American ones it was evolved quite independently and empirically by them and the teachers co-operating with them in seeking to impose coherence upon diverse researches of individual children.

10 On classroom group dynamics, *see* J. Fairley, *Patch History and Creativity* (1970), pp.79-81.

11 As K. Hudson emphasised in *Industrial Archaeology* (1962) and D.P. Dymond reiterated in *Archaeology for the Historian* (Historical Association, 1967), is it regrettable that in recent years archaeology has been equated in the popular mind with excavation. Archaeology is the study of physical evidence of all kinds.

5 WEALTH UNTOLD

> Almost everywhere important events are passed on by word of mouth from one generation to another . . . Each year that passes, something is lost or is changed and so becomes less correct. Fewer people realize the importance of handing on what they know to the next generation. Teachers must therefore do what they can to preserve the small and decreasing store of oral tradition.
>
> W.H. Laughton, *Teaching about our People* (1965), p.5.

BEFORE THE ADVENT of the mass media, conversation was much more important than it is today. Television and other forms of mass entertainment have tended to displace not only singing round the piano but the family circle talking round the fireside. Even a century after the beginning of the Industrial Revolution, many people still had jobs which allowed conversation to flow naturally throughout the working day, unimpeded by the noise of machinery or the enforced isolation of factory or office.

Conversation not only played a more important part in people's lives in the past; its subject matter was different too. In both town and country our grandparents knew much less than we do about the world, but much more about their immediate environment. Consequently, their conversation was, more often than not, restricted to family tradition and local life. Today, the average conversation is likely to be about television programmes, football matches, holidays or news items culled from the popular press. Teenagers have developed their own culture, mainly alienated from that of their elders. Nowadays, life changes so quickly that few young people feel they have anything to learn from Grandfather, whereas in the past, when skills were inherited from previous generations, the oral tradition in a family was inextricably bound up with learning a trade.[1] Furthermore, families now tend to be so dispersed, that in many cases the only opportunity to talk about ancestors and relatives is at christenings, weddings, funerals and at Christmas.

Personal Memories

In discussing imaginative writing, we have already seen how a child can be given an interest in the past if his attention is focussed upon a particular comprehensible situation, event or incident that is related to him personally through the participation of someone he knows. By questioning his relatives he may discover a view of the past unique to the individual who recalls it for him, totally unknown not only to other members of his class but to the teacher as well. Grandfather will remember points of detail which nobody has ever thought important enough to record, but which collectively help to recreate the atmosphere of the time. Here, for example, are an old lady's memories of Edwardian Lambeth (South London):

> . . . We had stalls all along the gutter in Wandsworth Road facing the shops. They were illuminated with flares attached to them and sold all kinds of merchandise, not forgetting the live eels which were in a small tank of water. No one bought dead eels — live ones were 8d. a pound — and it was surprising how clever the fishmonger was in catching them. I have seen one slither along the gutter with someone in pursuit, but this was unusual. They make very tasty eating with parsley sauce. We never bought a rabbit as people do now; they were there, propped up individually on the stall, in their skins and just split open down the front so that the buyer could examine what he was purchasing. We paid a great deal of attention to choosing which we thought was the best, and would look at several before parting with our 10d. or 1/-. The best ones of course, were the Ostend ones, which were a little dearer, but larger and quite superior to the English ones. We realised 2d. on the skin when we took it to the rag and bone shop which stood in Wilcox Road. Remembering the rabbits has reminded me of the offal shop where we could buy sheep's heads, tongues and brains, liver of all kinds, hearts, cowheel, lights — in fact anything to be got from the exterior or interior of animals, including joints of meat. These were obtained at the butchers (best sirloin 9d. a pound, other joints much cheaper), or at the pork butchers if pork was required. At Christmas time there would often be a live pig in the shop as an advertisement. There were stalls of infinite variety. One which stood outside Chapman's, the grocers and post office, was the sweet stall. Here the sweets were actually being made and sold and we could get a very great variety of boiled sweets at 4 ounces for a penny and actually warm when we took them home. We could stand and watch exactly what was put into the mixture and then see the sweet mixture pulled out and cut up into sizeable pieces.[2]

Tradition

Old people not only can tell us about the world of their youth, but may also be a storehouse of tradition going back 150 years. Here is one elderly gentleman's story about his great-grandfather, born in 1798.

> He was apprenticed to a watch and clockmaker, but finding his master harsh and tyrannical, ran away. As a result of his having failed to complete his apprenticeship to the watch and clockmaker, he was generally in poor circumstances throughout his life, and after his return to Olney he was glad to take charge of the Pound and to be responsible for straying cattle, the owners of which were required to pay one shilling before their animals were returned to them. He is said to have been called the 'howard'. One story concerning him and his duties is that he once found a straying donkey which belonged to a Romany woman named

Nancy Draper; Nancy was reputed to be a witch, and some of the townspeople strongly advised him to leave the donkey alone, lest he be bewitched. Their solemn warnings, however, had no effect, and notwithstanding any curses which Nancy gave expression to, she still had to pay the shilling fine before her animal was released.

The Pound over which he presided was situated not far from the Knoll in Olney High Street, and was a small round structure mostly of brick. My father always had a vivid recollection of it, for once, when he was quite a small boy, his grandfather, by way of a rough joke, put the little fellow into the Pound and locked the door. The boy was very frightened, and the image of the Pound was still keen in his mind at the end of his long life.[3]

Oral History Projects

Whether recounting their own memories or traditional ones, grandparents and great-grandparents will be able to give children information invaluable not only to the Family Historian, but also to the Local Historian, the Social Historian, the Business Historian or even, as Martin Middlebrook shows in his *The First Day on the Somme* (1971), to the student of Military History. Memories of kinship links may be as important to the Demographer as to the Genealogist or Family Historian; indeed, they can prove invaluable in charting patterns of migration. It is therefore surprising that, until recent years, little effort has been made systematically to record and collate the memories of old people. Many first-hand memories of 19th-century life are already lost. For example, we know a lot about how the Poor Law Guardians said they were running workhouses and a lot about what the Poor Law Commissioners thought of what the Poor Law Guardians were doing. We know next to nothing of what the inmates thought. Few 19th-century historians — and there were some very good ones — thought of recording this type of information for the benefit of their descendants. Similarly, it is unlikely that surviving documents for the Edwardian period will tell us all we want to know about that time.

George Ewart Evans has emphasised how 'in the process of talking with real people, facts and statistics take on a new significance'. He notes that the oral testimony of the 'people of the prior culture' can help those, such as sociologists or economists, who are primarily concerned with the present, and concludes: 'Most of all, oral testimony can help humanize those studies that appear to be suffering from an increasing mechanization, tending to give almost exclusive importance to processes, methods and statistics.'[4] It should be a task of historians and teachers to capture these memories and opinions (on tape if possible) before it is too late. The students of dialect and folk-song have, of course, been doing this for half a century,[5] but, with a few conspicuous exceptions like Evans, local and social historians have been so seduced by the wealth of documentary material surviving from the immediate past that they have tended to under-value oral evidence. The importance of tradition has been much more appreciated in emerging African nations, where written evidence is scanty and oral history is therefore doubly important. In *Teaching About Our People*, W.H. Laughton bases his Kenya history syllabus entirely upon oral tradition.[6] Nigeria, too, has taken a considerable interest in her unwritten history.[7] African oral tradition generally has been a happy hunting ground for anthropologists and ethnologists.[8] Oral History can be just as important, just as exciting and just as easily lost in England.

The situation in this country is at last changing, partly, no doubt, because of the increasing use of tape-recorders. In the early 1950s the British Institute of Recorded Sound was set up to establish a comprehensive national sound archive. Its main function is still to be a kind of British Museum Library for gramophone records and for books, periodicals and catalogues concerned with records and recording. However, as well as 160,000 discs, it holds 5,000 hours of tape and keeps a register of local collections of oral history tapes. In December 1969, the B.I.R.S. sponsored a day conference on Oral History at which an Oral History committee was set up. This committee started an occasional News Sheet, *Oral History*, which reports on work in progress. One of the most important Oral History projects is the *Interview Survey of Family Life and Work Experience before 1918*, directed by Dr. Paul Thompson of the Department of Sociology at the University of Essex. About 500 old people are being interviewed, the sample being derived from the 1911 Census of Occupations and distributed regionally through England, Scotland and Wales. There are questions on occupations, domestic routine, relationships with parents, punishment, leisure activities, religion, politics and education. All the tapes are being transcribed, and copies deposited in the British Institute of Recorded Sound.

Another Oral History project of particular interest to teachers is that undertaken by Prof. Theo Barker and John Whyman of Kent University Faculty of Social Sciences. School teachers are used as interviewers, and a number of conferences of teachers and university staff have been held. A brief questionnaire is used covering food, clothes, the home, health, school, shopping, leisure and relationships between parents and children. At Ruskin College, Oxford, Raphael Samuel has for several years organized a 'History Workshop', which is using oral evidence systematically, publishing the results in pamphlets. Edinburgh University School of Scottish Studies has over 3,000 tapes on Scottish oral tradition, folklore, dialect and folk-music, and the Department of Oral Traditions and Dialects at the Welsh Folk Museum, St. Fagans, Cardiff has a similar collection of Welsh material.[9] A number of libraries such as those of High Wycombe, Bucks., Darlington co. Durham or Tower Hamlets in London's East End have small, but steadily growing collections of tapes. So too have many museums such as the Museum of English Rural Life at Reading or the National Maritime Museum at Greenwich. The richest collection is, however, undoubtedly that of the B.B.C. which is at last open to researches. The written archives, consisting of about 7,500,000 pages of programme scripts are available at Caversham Park, Reading, by appointment with the Written Archives Officer, and at a fee of 50p per day or £5 per month. The sound archives at Broadcasting House can be used at a fee of £2 per day. Unfortunately, only about 1% of what goes on the air is kept, but this is superbly catalogued, often with synopses.[10]

In 1971 the theme of the Annual Conference of the Anthropological Section of the British Association was *Oral Tradition*, and in 1972, the Social Science Research Council organized a conference at Leicester University on *Problems of Oral History*. However, as yet there is still insufficient co-ordination in this field. For example, few of the interviewers take an interest in kinship links, and yet to the demographer concerned with migration or the sociologist concerned with the pattern of social relationships, these may be all important. Conversely, countless genealogists interview elderly relatives and confine their enquiries to occupations, dates, family moves and relationships. What is required is a well-endowed *Society for the Preservation of Oral and Kinship Evidence* (S.P.O.K.E.) to work in close liaison with the British Institute of Recorded Sound, the Historical Association, the Society of Genealogists, the Cambridge Group for the History of Population and Social Structure and other interested organizations. Only such a society can hope effectively to bring together the work of university departments of history, sociology, geography, anthropology, languages and music, of colleges of Education, of schools, of W.E.A. local history students, of Liberal Studies classes in technical colleges and Colleges of Further Education, and of an ever increasing number of amateur local historians, demographers and genealogists. All have their own limited objectives, but with a little direction many might be willing to go beyond these and collect material useful to others. At the very least, they could direct the attention of other workers to potentially fruitful sources of information.   Unless there is a really co-ordinated effort within the next 10 years, much of the oral tradition of our society will be lost forever. Despite all the exciting work that is being done, it seems likely that in many parts of the country our great-great-grandchildren may know little more about the life of the Common Man in the late 19th and early 20th centuries than we do about our 12th-century ancestors.

A Genealogical Reuter's Service

While men tend to be mainly concerned with their jobs, politics and sport, interest in family matters is more often a feminine preoccupation. Most families contain a matriarchal figure 'who provides a highly personalised computer-type service, sifting, sorting, arranging, re-aligning and distributing family news'. Thus, for Aunt Ann Forsyte, the family was her world:

> All their little secrets, illnesses, engagements and marriages, how they were getting on, and whether they were making money — all this was her property, her delight, her life: beyond this only a vague, shadowy mist of facts and persons of no real significance.[11]

It is not only the upper and middle classes who have their genealogical Reuter's service. In his study of London tenement families, Richard Firth discovered that women in early middle age were aware of family inter-relationships over five generations and, exceptionally, over seven. It was not uncommon for them to be able to count 200 kin.[12]

Because people are living longer as a result of a better standard of living and medical care, more and more families have four generations alive at one time: perhaps Great-grannie aged 83, Grannie aged 60, Mum aged 35 and the child aged 11.

Most great-grandparents know the names of their own grandparents, which gives some children a six-generation family history to work on. This takes the family back to an ancestor born about 1835, though a great-grandparent's memories, even when transmitting those of *his* parents or grandparents, will usually not stretch back more than a century. There are, however, many people still alive who can remember quite clearly Queen Victoria's Diamond Jubilee or the Boer War, and children should contact as many elderly relatives as possible, either personally or by letter, in order to discover as much information as they can.

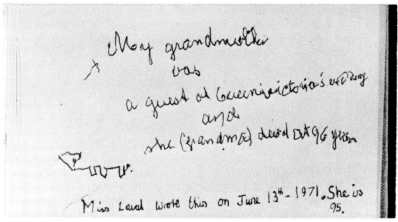

Plate 8. A Living Link with the Young Victoria
Miss Laval clearly remembers her grandmother's eye-witness account of the Queen's wedding in 1840

A surprising amount of tradition can emerge from the most un-likely source. In 1956, one of the authors interviewed a boot repairer in London's Caledonian Road. He knew nothing of his family's background and all his father, a milk roundsman, was able to do was to refer the enquirer to his aunt, an old lady of 86 living in North London. However, a visit to her proved very fruitful. She pointed to an oil portrait on the wall saying this was her great-grandfather, who, subsequent research showed, had been born in 1770. He was, she said, a small country builder who secured the contract to build a stately home, where he retired to end his days as gatekeeper. (He appears as such in the 1851 Census). In the 1830s, his son went to London, where he engaged, very profitably, in speculative building in what were then the London suburbs. The descendants of his elder sons have remained prosperous. His youngest son was the father of a copper-plate writer, the grand-father of the milk roundsman and great-grandfather of the boot repairer.

Tracing Distant Relatives

Some of the genealogical information given by elderly relatives will be very vague. For example, Grannie may say, 'I remember as a child visiting my grandmother in Lowestoft — more than likely my cousins are still living there, although we haven't been in touch for forty years'. The teacher can discuss with the children the ways in which such relatives can be contacted, for if they are still alive, they may, besides contributing useful memories, possess a Family Bible or other documents. They are likely to remember Great-great-grandmother much better than Grannie does, as they lived in the same town, whereas she saw her grandmother rarely. Furthermore, they may be able to put the child in touch with yet other relatives. If the children have caught the genealogical bug, and are prepared to spend a fair amount of their own time upon the project, there are nearly always slender clues to work on — an address on a letter of 1925 or a memory of being given dinner by affluent relatives before leaving for Australia in the early 1920s. Such clues should be followed up by visits or searches in telephone directories, voters' lists or street directories. When a letter to an out-of-date address is returned 'Gone Away' or 'Not known at this address', another letter to 'The Occupier' of a neighbouring house asking for help sometimes elicits a helpful reply. In some cases, although the neighbour is a newcomer to the district she has asked her neighbours and found someone who can give the required information.

This is a kind of detective work which has an appeal to some older children, and running one's quarry to earth provides consider-able satisfaction, quite irrespective of the value of the information obtained. One of the authors has, by a variety of different means, traced several hundred relatives.

Types of Information

There are three basic kinds of information which the children can obtain from talking to old people: *genealogical, biographical* and more generally *historical.* Obviously these are very closely linked. However, it is best to confine each interview as far as possible to the collection of only one kind of information. If the pupils first concentrate on collecting genealogical data, this will provide them with a framework of names, dates and places. These dry bones can later be given flesh and blood by the addition of bibliographical detail and, finally, the more generally historical information will clothe the family figures with their social contexts.

Interview Techniques

In practice all these and many other kinds of information are likely to be offered in one interview. Children will find it difficult to organise this material. They will need to be helped to ask precise questions on limited topics, to be prepared to deal with unexpected answers and to be encouraged to develop the confidence, quick thinking and background knowledge necessary to enable them to elicit useful information from the inarticulate, to exploit that unexpectedly offered and to sift that given in rambling, incoherent answers. Peter Townsend writes of one of his interviews in the East End:

> One man in his late seventies said, 'When people come here they think they are going to meet a tottering old man. But by the time I've finished with them they've said very little, and I've said a lot.' This, alas, was only too true. The first interview lasted three-and-a half hours. It was impossible to keep him to the point. A question whether he liked reading would lead on to historical studies, Queen Elizabeth the First, whether she was a virgin and whether red-haired women were often virgins. In the course of the interview he touched on how much money Tottenham Hotspur had in the bank, whether Gordon Richards was a real jockey, the iniquities of American tariffs, whether Ernest Bevin had deserved the credit he got for his work for the dock labourers, how his father used to buy Russian ponies, and why Keir Hardie had died of a broken heart.[13]

Faced by such an interviewee, any researcher might be at a loss!

Before the class attempts such interviewing therefore, their teacher should play a tape-recording of an interview and discuss with his pupils the suitability of the questions asked and the value of the information received. The recording may be made by a child — perhaps one of those hampered by a family problem — or by the teacher himself. In neither case need the interview be of B.B.C.

standard. A poor one is more likely to draw the children's attention to probable pitfalls.

While few children will attain the skill of a professional interviewer, their performance can be much improved if a systematic attempt is made to teach them interviewing techniques. This is best done through a series of dialogues in which one child takes the part of the interviewer, another that of the old man or woman.

The Reluctant Confidant

In *Where Beards Wag All*, George Ewart Evans noted that rural East Anglians show what might be interpreted by a questioner as suspicion or evasiveness. One Suffolk farmer confided:

> Then there's a dislike of being questioned. I don't think it's resentment exactly so much as a reluctance to come down definitely and make any kind of overt stand — unless they know you very well indeed. They won't do that. They'll shuffle and hedge. And that's not through any weakness of character or indecision on their part. I don't quite know what it stems from. They are cagey and not at all eager to let anyone else know their business, especially if they have a bit of good fortune. They'll conceal that at all costs. I suppose that's the attitude of the peasant, really. When he gets a little bit of something — well! I include myself here. I'm a peasant! and I think you're frightened of tempting fate if you've got something good or had a bit of luck. Or on the other hand, the landlord may get to know about it and stick the rent up. That would be a lot worse![14]

This cageyness may be a regional characteristic rather than a rural one. In any case, children interviewing their elderly relatives are in a more favourable position than are strangers. Moreover elderly people seem to be less reticent with children than with adults, perhaps because they are less suspicious of an ulterior motive. Nevertheless, some cases of reticence will undoubtedly occur. When they do, one would be sensible to heed Evans's advice, the fruit of long experience:

> If I knew an informant well and he knew and appreciated what I was about, I did not hesitate to use a notebook. But if I suspected that the sight of a notebook would dry up information at the source, I memorized the salient points of a conversation; wrote up the interview as soon as I could; and if I was in doubt about some aspect of it or wanted fuller information, returned repeatedly until I got it right.[15]

Recording

Many children, particularly younger ones, will have great difficulty in recording the answers: some write very slowly and laboriously, and even if the main questions are written down, they will find it difficult to compress both supplementary questions and the answers to them into notes.

They will need to keep the questions and answers fairly short, so that the really important points are written down in an orderly sequence. This is by no means easy. Often the person interviewed will launch out into a fascinating anecdote, which it would be not only discourteous, but frequently impossible for an adult, let alone a child, to divert. All the child can do in such circumstances is to listen carefully, and when he has the opportunity to write down as much as he remembers, afterwards giving Grandad the account to read or reading it to him. This is a principle with a wider application: as far as possible the reports should be read back to the person interviewed.

The child should keep a log of every item of information he discovers, together with its source. This is important training in the handling of evidence; otherwise if the rough notes taken at the interviews have been destroyed, the child may have no idea which relative provided any particular piece of information.

Genealogical information is best recorded (in the log book) in the form of mini family trees. It should include dates and places of births, marriages and deaths, occupations and places of residence. This is itself a useful exercise, as it involves the obtaining and recording of information. Although the greatest degree of precision should be aimed at, often calculations will be necessary to arrive at an approximate date (Great-grandfather died about 1947 aged about 75). It is important that only the information obtained from a particular relative is entered so that the source can be accurately identified. For example, if Grandfather knows his aunt Deborah married someone called Mattock, but does not know the Christian name, the latter should be left blank, even if the child knows from interviewing another relative that his name was John. This is because genealogical information obtained orally is often inaccurate. When one of the authors began his own genealogical investigations, he was told quite categorically his great-grandmother's name was Sarah. It turned out to be Martha.

All the genealogical information known to a person should be obtained at once, even if there is no immediate intention of studying several families. Thus at any rate the genealogical basis of the Family History will be secured. Elderly relatives have a habit of dying before follow-up visits can be made.

Tape Recordings

Just as the widespread home use of cine-cameras enables family events to be recorded on celluloid, so some children may be fortunate enough to have access to school or family tape-recorders. They will be in a position to do what has been impossible in all other periods of history — record the actual voices of their informants. As A.J.P. Taylor has stressed:

Until recently our knowledge of the past was mostly second-hand: records by one man of what he and others said and did. Now we have recording instruments for both sight and sound and they preserve the past for us in a new, more direct way . . . Historians should use these records much more than they have done so far.[16]

Plates 9 and 10.   Tape-recording Grandma's memories of school (1907)
(Grandma is third from the left)

Even when memories are captured on the tape, the information will still need to be put into a more easily accessible form. A suggested procedure for older children is: recording session; brief summary in log book; editing (i.e. transferring from one tape to another with a commentary); making reference cards.

Unpublished Memoirs

Although the task of interviewing has considerable educational value, if the teacher wishes to place the emphasis upon obtaining as much information as possible, he can ask the children to try to persuade their relatives to write their memoirs. To encourage this, he can duplicate questionnaires, with adequate spaces for the answers.

Some parents and grandparents will need little prompting and will write, and in many cases type, extensively and fluently. Here, for example, are school memories of the late 1920s from the autobiography of the mother of a secondary school pupil.

> Discipline was on the whole much more strict at school, and the teacher's word was law. This was even more noticeable at primary school. Even in the first class, we sat at our own desks and were

taught by the teacher sitting at her desk in front of the class. Great emphasis was put on the three 'R's', reading, writing and arithmetic. We had dictation every day, frequent spelling tests and spelling bees, and mental arithmetic tests. By the time we left

Plate 11. 'The teacher's word was law . . . we sat at our own desks'

the infant classes for the junior school, we were expected to be able to punctuate properly and use capital letters in the right places, and most of us could do so. Every day we had time for 'silent' reading, and the teachers also read aloud to us regularly. Even at grammar school, the needlework teacher read to us while we sat quietly and sewed. We tackled much more advanced books than young children do now, and by the time I left junior school, I had read much of Dickens, as well as many other English and French classics. Altogether, I think we had a much better basic education at primary school than children of today. However, at grammar school, although the syllabus was much the same as today, I think we probably did not cover quite as much ground. We lived a much more sheltered existence, and were not encouraged to take much interest in the world around us. Outside activities were frowned on and the only school clubs I can remember were a Bible study group and a cycling and rambling club.[17]

Class Card-Index

There is no reason why more general historical information collected by one child should not be shared by all in a spirit of friendly co-operation. A classroom card-index will usually prove the most convenient way of recording such information for the benefit of all.

A child studying *food*, for example, may well derive information about eating habits which has been collected from the families of

many other children. This could provide much of his source material. Making such cards also appeals to children's natural desire to
collect, arrange and record.

8 ins. x 6 ins. has proved the most convenient size for the index
cards. To ensure that any particular one can be found easily, they
should be arranged alphabetically, a single card normally being
devoted to a single topic. As the index grows, children may be introduced to more complicated indexing systems. For example, it is
probable that with a topic like food, on which much information
may be collected, it will soon be necessary to have cards headed:

FOOD: BREAKFAST

> *FOOD: BREAKFAST*   *about 1900*
>
> *Occupation (Father's): Cab driver*
>
> *District: Lambeth, South London.*
> *Eggs and Bacon or Fish (herring, kippers) might*
> *be preceded by porridge made with oatmeal*
> *bought loose. Tea to drink. Children had milk*
> *and water.*
>
> *Name and Age of Informant: Mrs. A.E.F. Steel – 77*
>
> *Name of Contributor: D.J. Steel   Date: 22.11.68.*

The card index may contain a lot of information on a variety of
topics, contributed by members of the present or former classes.
Children should be taught to check such information wherever
possible, by reference to books, trade catalogues, or newspaper
advertisements.

Drawing Conclusions

By pooling their information the pupils can build up a more
coherent picture of life in the past. For example, the reports of
third form boys in a Reading secondary school[18] showed that most
of their parents were of working-class origin, and the socio-
economic watershed for many families seems to have been the last
war. Most of the children were astonished at the extent and depth
of poverty in the town revealed by the majority of the reports for
the childhood of the parents, and for most of the lives of grandparents and great-grandparents. In their grandfathers' time, luxuries
were few and far between, and even many necessities had to be
carefully saved for. There are numerous mentions of pig clubs,
dress clubs, Christmas clubs and such like. For example:

> At 14 my maternal grandmother had left school and was working
> as a home-help to a middle-class family, which meant that she

actually lived with the family and got 1/6 - 2/- pocket money
with all meals provided. She saved 6d. of it on a dress club, put
2½d. towards a Bible club which was the only equivalent to a
Youth Club there was. She moved with this family to a house
that had electricity and this was a marvellous thing. At a touch of
a switch on came a light which took some getting used to!

My paternal grandmother lived in the Midlands where she and
her parents were servants in the same great house. She used to
get £5 3s. 0d. a year plus her keep and to earn this she worked
5 a.m. to 5 p.m. Her first job in the morning was to light the
heaters so that the others could get up in the warm. She also did
jobs like polishing the brass, emptying the toilets and, sometimes,
helping her father do the gardening.

Children were expected to work hard in the home:

Like my mother's youth my grandmother's was very strict. She had
to perform even more duties than my mother as both parents
worked from 7.00 to 6.00. She had to do all the housework along
with her five sisters and five brothers. They had breakfast very
early, about 6.30, or did not have it at all. They then went to
school. In the evening they came home about 5.00 and did the
other jobs; e.g. feeding animals, digging the garden etc. They then
had tea and washed up. Then, if no other jobs needed doing
they could go out to play.

The stern unbending Victorian paterfamilias was still very much
the rule until the Second World War.

As a boy he was always getting into trouble, scrumping apples
etc. This he used to do with his brothers. His father was very strict
and he was quite often getting the strap or stick from his Dad.

Father was not only to be feared after 'criminal' activities. His
attitude often pervaded every aspect of family life, as the following
extract shows:

My paternal grandfather was born in 1890 and went to a local
school at Guildford where he was until the age of fourteen, when
he went to Farnham to work as a brickmaker. He lived at home
and on weekdays he left the house for work about eight and
worked solidly until seven in the evenings. His father was a very
hard man and if my grandfather murmured a word at the table
he was severely punished. The same happened to him if he talked
back to his parents. His father worked very hard to support six
growing children.

They had a very good evening meal which was usually meat as
my grandfather's father also bred and sold rabbits for the table.
Even at twenty-six he had to be in bed by ten. No grace was said
at table.

Quite a few times my grandfather ran away from home, but
when he returned he often wished he hadn't done so. On Sundays
they always had rabbit stew and he had to sit for at least one
hour. Once every other Sunday the family had to go and see
their grandparents who only lived a few streets away. They had
tea there, stayed until about ten o'clock when they went home
to bed.

Another point which comes over very clearly is the paucity of amusements, particularly in the countryside:

> Saturday was pay day for my grandparents and, if they felt like it, they used to go to the pub and get drunk as they had nothing better to do.

The infrequency of holidays is a constant theme, though some grandparents remember staying with relatives or going out for day trips. These were obviously memorable occasions:

> My paternal grandmother used occasionally to go out for day trips. When she went out on these she can remember using one of the bathing machines and being ducked under by men who were paid to do this. These men did this because in those times (1904) it was believed that sea-water was good for you and that the more of you you got under the water the healthier you could stay.

In the country, attendance at church and Sunday school was, in the grandparents' childhood, almost universal. In the towns, though many more children attended Church than do today, there was a markedly lower attendance. An excuse given by some families was that they were too poor to afford Sunday clothes.

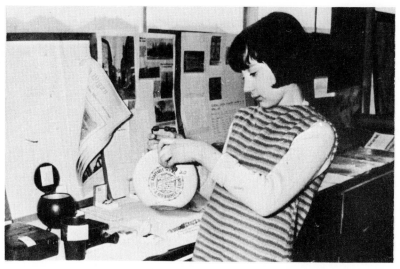

Plate 12. This child's grandmother worked as a pit-born lass, sorting coal at the age of 12. The stone hot-water bottle dates from 1878. (St. Cuthbert's Junior School, Wigan)

From the mass of material that these Reading third formers collected and collated, it was clear that many of them had found Oral History more interesting and relevant than more traditional forms of school history.

Notes and References

1   *See* George Ewart Evans, *Where Beards Wag All* (1970), Part I; and George Sturt, *The Wheelwright's Shop* (1958).

2   The late Mrs. A.E.F. Steel, recorded 1969.

3   The authors are grateful to Mr. Ralph Kitchener of Tewin, Herts., for permission to reproduce this story.

4   George Ewart Evans, *op. cit.*, p.20.

5   On the historical importance of folk songs, *see* Michael Pollard, 'Oral Tradition and Local History', in *The Local Historian*, vol. 9, no. 7 (1971), pp.343-347, and R. Copper, *A Song for Every Season* (1971).

6   This interesting book, written to implement the 1962 Kenyan History and Civics syllabus, was perhaps the first to abandon a traditional 'content' syllabus in favour of an environmental approach based on oral and kinship evidence.

7   *See*, for example, S.O. Biobaku, 'The Problem of Traditional History with Special reference to Yoruba Traditions', in *Journal of the Historical Society of Nigeria*, vol. 1 (1956) pp.43-47 and the same author's 'The Wells of African History, in *West African Review*, vol. 40, no. 304 (1953), pp.18-19.

8   *See* Jan Vansina, *Oral Tradition* (1965). This book, which is mainly based on the author's work in Rwanda, has an extensive bibliography.

9   Detailed lists of Oral History projects in progress have been published in Numbers 1 and 2 of *Oral History*, edited by Paul Thompson, Department of Sociology, University of Essex, Colchester, Essex, and distributed by the British Institute of Recorded Sound, 29 Exhibition Rd., London, S.W.7.

10   For more information on both the Written and the Sound archives see Paul Thompson, 'The B.B.C. Archives', *Oral History*, No. 2 (1972), pp. 11-18.

11   J. Galsworthy, *The Man of Property*, Penguin edn. (1957), p.22.

12   See R. Firth (ed.), *Two Studies of Kinship in London*, Department of Anthropology, London School of Economics, Monographs on Social Anthropology, No. 15 (1956).

13   Peter Townsend, *The Family Life of Old People*, abridged Pelican edn. (1963), p.28.

14   George Ewart Evans, *op. cit.*, p.181.

15   *Ibid.*, pp. 23-24.

16   A.J.P. Taylor, *English History, 1914-1945*, Penguin edn. p.736.

17   Memories supplied by a first former at Maiden Erlegh School, Berks.

18   Stoneham School, Reading.

6 THE ATTIC ARCHIVIST

Truth, that shy Truth, that we run panting after through the halls of State and the drawing rooms, often turns out to have secreted herself after all, in an old trunk in the attic.

R.J. Cruikshank, *Charles Dickens and Early Victorian England* (1949), p.1.

IN THE COURSE of conversation, the relatives of nearly every child will produce birth, marriage and death certificates, funeral cards, family Bibles and other similar records.

A little prompting may also encourage relatives to unearth old letters, diaries, newspaper cuttings, old Service documents (including Prisoner of War papers), passports and notebooks and papers of all kinds. Children undertaking Family History projects have even brought in 18th-century records, including a recipe book, a manuscript book of medicinal remedies, and apprenticeship indentures. Such heirlooms may be scattered amongst numerous relatives, or have descended in a single collection to a distant cousin with whom the child's immediate family is not in touch. It is thus worth emphasising that the parents should be encouraged to help the child to follow up clues as to the whereabouts of distant relations, and to examine all relevant material. Of course, the range and quantity of this varies enormously from family to family, not only because of differing social and educational backgrounds, but because the destruction or preservation of such documents is very much a matter of choice.

Letters

Although letters are the commonest of family documents, they do not often feature in the average Family History project, for many parents are, understandably, reluctant to allow their children to bring them to school. Many children have, however, been allowed to use such letters at home and to copy or refer to them in their Family Histories. Of those which have been brought to school, perhaps the most moving was a pencilled letter from a soldier at the Front in 1918. Written a few days before the Armistice, it describes the grim conditions in the author's sector and expresses the hope that there was some truth in the rumour that the war would soon be ended.

One student at an Adult Evening Institute class had a very fine collection of letters, including a series written in the 1890s by James Morpeth, a Scottish farmer, to his nephew, a soft furnisher in London. Concerned mainly with a farmer's daily life and recreations (especially horse-racing), they epitomise the two major Victorian pre-occupations; religion and death. Family bereavements are described at inordinate length, the details of the death-bed

Plate 13. Birth, Baptism, Marriage, Work and School Certificates
(St. Cuthbert's Primary School, Wigan)

Plate 14. Checking Birth Certificates with Family Bible
(St. Cuthbert's Primary School, Wigan)

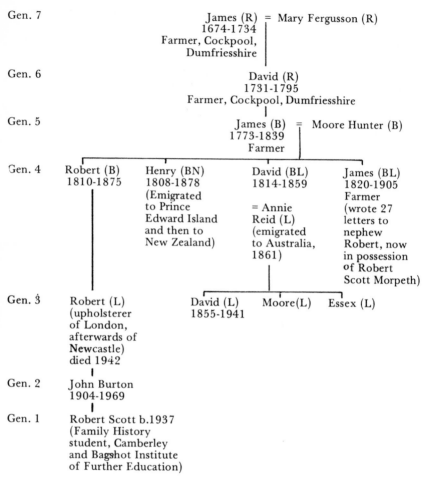

Gen. 7   James (R) = Mary Fergusson (R)
                                          1674-1734
                                       Farmer, Cockpool,
                                       Dumfriesshire

Gen. 6   David (R)
                                               1731-1795
                                    Farmer, Cockpool, Dumfriesshire

Gen. 5   James (B) = Moore Hunter (B)
                                          1773-1839
                                            Farmer

Gen. 4   Robert (B)   Henry (BN)   David (BL)   James (BL)
          1810-1875   1808-1878   1814-1859   1820-1905
                          (Emigrated   Farmer
                          to Prince   = Annie   (wrote 27
                          Edward Island   Reid (L)   letters to
                          and then to   (emigrated   nephew
                          New Zealand)   to Australia,   Robert, now
                                            1861)   in possession
                                                              of Robert
                                                              Scott Morpeth)

Gen. 3   Robert (L)   David (L)   Moore(L)   Essex (L)
          (upholsterer   1855-1941
          of London,
          afterwards of
          Newcastle)
          died 1942

Gen. 2   John Burton
          1904-1969

Gen. 1   Robert Scott b.1937
          (Family History
          student, Camberley
          and Bagshot Institute
          of Further Education)

                              KEY: R = mentioned in rent book
                                     L = wrote, received or appea
                                         in letters in possession o
                                         Robert Scott Morpeth
                                     N = mentioned in newspaper
                                         cutting
                                     B = appears in Family Bible
                                         entries (not quoted)

                        MORPETH PEDIGREE

scene embellished with appropriate expressions of religious senti-
ment. The correspondence reflects the letter-writer's not uncommon
delusion that the recipient is interested in the minute intimacies of
his or her ailments.

Although the older student will find such letters help him
to understand the psychology of his Victorian great-grandparents,
to a child they are just 'plain boring'. Much more interesting from
his point of view are those letters which tell a dramatic story. Here
for example, is another letter from the same Morpeth collection
which few teachers could fail to exploit with great success. The
writer, Annie Morpeth, a young widow (see pedigree), was sailing
with her three children to seek a new life in Australia.

> On board the ship Felorine,
> 21st Feb. 1861.

My Dear James,

   We are now within a few hours sail of Melbourne, having got
the pilot on board in the morning, and I can scarcely express how
thankful I feel to God, for preserving and keeping us in perfect
health, and preserving us from all the dangers of the great deep.
The Captain will go on shore in his boat whenever we come to
anchorage. I dare say I will go with him, and see Mrs. Lawrence if
it should be only for a few minutes. I will take David with me and
leave the two children in charge of a young person who has been
most kind and attentive to them and me. As the mail leaves
Melbourne the day after tomorrow, and as I know you would be
anxious to hear of our safe arrival, I think it best not to trust till
tomorrow, as the excitement of landing might prevent me from

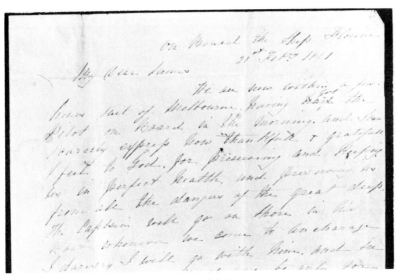

Plate 15. Annie's Letter

getting it done. I know you will be all delighted to hear that we have had a first-rate passage of 94 days, which is very quick considering how she is laden, and also being a slow sailing vessel besides, we have had beautiful weather, and favourable winds almost all the way, with the exception of few rough days, within the past week. You will be glad to learn that the children are in excellent health. Little Essie is much improved, but she was very poorly for four or five weeks after leaving home. Poor child, she cut 10 teeth after coming on board, which both reduced her very much and made her very peevish, but for the last two months she has been improving every day, and is a great favourite with the Captain and indeed with everyone. David and Moore are both getting very tall, they have been good children, and have given me very little trouble. David was a little sick for two days when we were getting out of the channel, but for Moore I may say she was not half an hour sick all the time. Mr. McLean has been most exceedingly kind and attentive to me, and indeed everyone on board. I may say I have been as much attended as if I had been a cabin passenger, but I could never had done as a steerage passenger, had I not been so fortunate to fall in with such kind people. I was never sick, and enjoyed much better health than I did all the time I was in Scotland. The only thing that I suffered from was my head, but I have much cause for thankfulness that I have stood the passage so well, and they all say that I look much better than I did when I left home. This is a most beautiful day, and everyone is busier than another, but I have everything in order, only I feel that I am scarcely able to write. I feel very anxious to hear how you are all at home, also particularly Mr. and Mrs. Sloane. The children often talk of the whole of you, also of Uncle John Phillips and Aunt Mary. Grandpa and Grandma are often talked about, and also Anne, Jane and Janet. Little Essex always concludes, with awa, awa. I will not have time to write any one by this mail, but yourself, so perhaps you would drop a few lines to Jessie, Mrs. Lachlan and Mrs. and Mr. Dougall's people, for I know they will be all very anxious to hear of our safe arrival. If all well, and spared till next mail, I shall write you and all my other friends. I would have done so by this one if it had not been leaving so soon. I trust Mrs. Morpeth, Robert John and yourself are all well, and I will write to you all particulars if spared. I have found the Captain most attentive and kind, and would never desire a better Commander had I the same passage to go at any future time. He seems a thorough seaman, and has not had bad spirits for upwards of 7 years. He is now only 8 and 20 years of age. David and he are great friends, and he often teases David about returning with him. He sometimes seems half inclined to do so, the master is a nice man, and has been exceedingly kind to the children. You must excuse as I scarcely know whether my head is off or on,

With best and kindest love to one and all.

I remain, My Dear James,

Your ever affectionate sister,

Annie Morpeth

One cannot but suspect that the young widow had another aim in view besides emigration — was the young and virile sea captain aware of his own attractions?

Diaries

Relatively few diaries have come to light during Family History Projects. Apart from the fact that, like letters, they might be considered too personal or valuable to entrust to children, there may be two other reasons why they are so scarce. The first is that the historical and sociological value of a diary may not be appreciated after the death of its writer, so that the diary is either destroyed or passes to a distant relative. Secondly, fewer people may have kept diaries than is commonly imagined. Where children have brought diaries, these have thrown personal attitudes into bold relief. Not only do they usually provide interesting examples of national, political or religious bias but they may betray feelings which were not confided even to the diarist's closest friends.

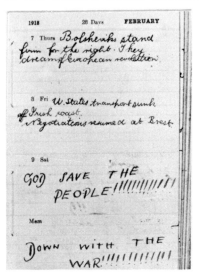

Two Political Diaries

Plate 16. Chartists, 1848   Plate 17. Bolsheviks, 1918

Sometimes they reveal opinions about the conduct of wars or contemporary political events which the writers might have hesitated to voice abroad. In order for the teacher to show the preoccupations of a diarist, it is helpful if he compares the entries with those in another diary for the same dates. A teacher is very fortunate if the same class can supply two diaries for the same period, but it should not be difficult for him to find a published one. The following extracts come from two unpublished diaries for 1918, the first written by a sergeant at the Front and the second by a teacher's friend who had been a highly emancipated and politically active lady member of the Independent Labour Party.

Sunday 24 Feb.   Nothing doing. To
                    Reninghelst to tea.

We heard Ex-Private Simmons
on 'The War, the I.L.P. and
the future'. He is the best
chap yet, I think — awful
revolutionary too. Then we
went to say goodbye to Fraser.

Monday 25 Feb.   Nothing to do. Beth!
                   Très bien. Line
                   tomorrow!!

Tues. 26 Feb.   In line. In support.
                   MENIN ROAD.

News is coming through about
Russia. Lenin and Trotzky
have been disagreeing. Lenin
for peace — Trotzky for
defending the revolution by
force of arms. Lenin wins
and the Bolskeviks accept
German terms but the Germans
are still advancing, and the
Bolsheviks are calling the
people to arms.

Wed. 27 Feb.   Staff officer killed by
                   my side at 9.00 a.m.

Thurs. 28 Feb.   Fairly quiet.
                   Reconnoitring on top in
                   daylight — Reconnoitred
                   shell hole posts with
                   Charles.

GOD SAVE RUSSIA!

Fri. 1 March   3 a.m. Bombarded by
                   Gas Shell Barrage. 3 p.m.
                   by 59's. No casualties.
                   Relieved D. Coy. left
                   of MENIN ROAD.
                   Ftg. [Fighting] Patrol.

Went to first branch
meeting of I.L.P. Fine
sport!!

Sat. 2 Mar.   Things fairly quiet except
                   for T.M.s and Gas shells.
                   Reconnoitring Patrol.
                   Fritz nearly snaffled me.
                   — Large Patrols on this
                   Sector.

About this time we are
officially told of the Japanese
intervention in Russia. Of
course we socialists had heard
rumours for a long time.

Sun. 3 Mar   Very quiet all day.
                   Cracked my knee by
                   Shell at 7.45 p.m.
                   Carried down.

Went to meeting only and
then slacked.

Mon. 4 Mar.   To 48th F.A. and after
                   Lunch to No. 2. loan
                   C.C.S. Leg in splints.

Bolsheviks definitely accept
peace terms — rotten ones I
think. But who can blame
the poor chaps whatever they

Tues. 5 Mar.   X-rays and sent to Base.
                   No. 1 R.C. Hos. Paris
                   Plage — Out 10.30 p.m.

do? They have made a brave
stand to the best of their
ability.

Wed. 6 Mar.   Splints on. Early day.
                   Doc. says stay in bed.

Rumania is making peace
apparently.

Thurs. 7 Mar.   Doc. says 'Blighty'. Some
                   excitement.

The Russians are evacuating
Petrograd in case of German
advance although they have
made peace. What is the
meaning of the Japanese
intervention?????

Apprentice Indentures

As apprenticeship is still very strong in many trades and industries, indentures are found in fairly large numbers. These can be very useful from a genealogical point of view. Thus Thomas Hulme, (Plate 18) was born in 1837 and his father in 1812.

Plate 18. An Apprentice Indenture

Indentures such as this also pose all kinds of interesting historical questions. Did the apprentice live at home or in his master's house? What were the conditions under which he served? And there may also be more specific queries. Why was Thomas apprenticed to a gold-case maker? A little research will soon reveal that Clerkenwell was the district in London most noted for watch and clock making. An obvious follow-up question is *why*?

Household and Business Records

Other important categories of personal documents are old household and business papers. Once again, families may be reluctant to allow children to take these to school. However, bills, account books and other records of payment can provide a wealth of comparative data on such things as wages, prices, household budgets, patterns of expenditure and levels of consumption. Children will often express great surprise at how low prices were as recently as World War II. It is, of course, important when discussing prices to relate them to the wages of the time.

Really old account books are rare, but here is an entry from a rent book which runs from 1729 to 1774. It was used to record the

rent of a farm called Cockpool in Dumfriesshire to the factor of
Viscount Stormont, who lived in Cumlogan Castle. The rent payers
were successively James Morpeth (1674-1734), his widow, Mary
Fergusson, and their son David (1731-1795). (See page 70.)

> Cumlogan the 15th day of May 1736 years. Received from David
> Morpeth in Cockpool, fifty six pounds Eighteen shillings and
> six pennies Scots money, and that in full and complete payment
> of his Rent for the Croft and Year 1735, and therefore the same
> is hereby discharged by me factor for the Viscount of Stormont.
>
> Jo. Carruthers.

Certificates

Most families proudly hoard a
bewildering variety of certificates.
Many are for academic prowess and
the diversity of the examinations
and examining authorities may well
surprise those brought up on the
11 plus, 16 plus and 18 plus
hurdles. Others are for vocational
skills such as shorthand and technical
drawing or for sports and recreations such as swimming and danc-
ing, singing and playing the piano.
Not all the certificate winners were
relatives; some were prize heifers,
horses or dogs!

Born 22 Feb 1924

Goddess of Beauty by Cloth of Gold
of Queen of the South

Plates 19 and 20. Not all certificate winners were relatives!

Plate 21. A Diversity of Examinations

Plate 22. Skills

Plate 23. Sports

Applications, Testimonials and References

Grandparents and great-grandparents lived in an age when servants were much more numerous than today, and when a servant without a reference was a servant without a job. Some families have kept copies of forms or letters applying for jobs. These can be invaluable, as they often provide a potted biography of the applicant, as well as clues to interests, aptitudes and activities. Occasionally even an original application which was never despatched may survive. Perhaps the ancestor thought better of it. (See Plate 24.) Teachers may find food for thought in the fact that in 1914 a trained certificated teacher of three years' standing was earning the princely salary of £80 a year. Equally interesting is the candidate's own school career. Her scholarship to a Grammar

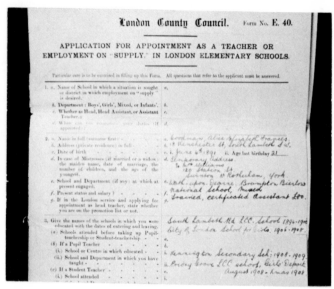

Plate 24. Undespatched application

School was for two years only, after which she has to transfer to a less prestigious school.

Birthday and Christmas Cards

Old birthday and Christmas cards are common; embroidered ones may date from Victorian times. A collection of these can be displayed, mounted on photographic hinges. If the cards which can be dated are arranged in chronological sequence, children in the class may be provided with useful evidence for dating those for which they have no provenance. One may ask, 'When were cards first produced? Why? What are the traditional scenes?'

Picture Postcards

Many homes have quite large collections of old picture post-cards. These not only evoke the atmosphere of a period, but often portray scenes that have since vanished almost without trace. The postmark on the back will often help to date the scene. Not all postcards will be of views. One pupil, for example, brought to school some interesting postcards lampooning the suffragettes and another, one of peace celebrations at Woking. With postcards, as with photographs, the pupil may need help in interpreting them.

Plate 25. World War I greetings card

Plate 26. Anti-Suffragette postcard

Archive Consciousness

An archivist's recognition of documents is usually determined by their age, their rarity or the family's social standing. A modern. rent book would not be accepted by most local archivists, and yet a cross-section of rent books for a large number of streets might be invaluable to a future economic historian, for it would give a human dimension to the reports and statistics in the Housing Department's records which, in any case, may not survive successive municipal weedings.

Archive consciousness should be taught as a part of conservation. Children can then play their part in preventing the wanton destruction of documents which often takes place after the death of an older member of a family. As we have seen, one of the premises of Family History is that if a child is unable to 'feel history' in the context of his own family, he is unlikely to feel it anywhere else.

The Archive Code

Just as we need a S.P.O.K.E. to preserve oral evidence (see p.54) so we need a nationally recognised *Archive Code* on analogous lines to the *Country Code*. Although space is a major factor in deciding what can be preserved, many houses have attics where there is ample room for small boxes. If present members of families are uninterested in their 'archives', their grandchildren may be very grateful for the legacy. If parents feel unable to find room for family records, there are many librarians and archivists who will be pleased to receive letters, account books, postcards and photographic collections. Where old family documents are treasured, the teacher can ask the parents for permission to photocopy them and, if they are of exceptional interest, copies should be made for the local record office. It is important that confidence should not be betrayed. One grandmother allowed the authors to photocopy her deceased husband's diaries for 1916 and 1918. Some time later, she expressed reservations about the confidential nature of some of the material, so the authors gave her their copies, asking her to destroy any she did not wish to become public property. In the end, no sheets were destroyed.

Using the Documents

The documents children bring to school often pose more questions than they answer. For example, one of the documents that children frequently are allowed to bring to school is their father's or grandfather's discharge book. Here they can verify what they already know, i.e. that Dad has brown hair, brown eyes, has a mole on his left forearm, is five foot eight tall and served in the Blankshire Regt., first as a private then as a sergeant for five years from 1940 to 1945. They might also discover that he was considered a 'trustworthy soldier with plenty of initiative'. However, it does not take them long to realise that there is much more to their father than the profile portrayed in the document. Likewise, although it records he was wounded, it does not say how or where; it states that he served in Burma, but gives no details of the campaigns he fought in; nor does it say anything about whether he wanted to fight at all, or what his attitude to the war was. Once the child begins to think about what is written down on the one hand, and what is omitted on the other, he is stimulated to further inquiries. In this case he can ask Dad more questions. Older children can consult the history of the regiment or even visit the regimental museum if it is a local one.

A Documentary Series

The Morpeth family documents already quoted illustrate the immense power a few documents can have in building up a Family History. In the Family tree (p.70) information about Generations 1, 2 and 3 is derived from parents and certificates, Generations 3 and 4 from letters; Generations 4 and 5 from Family Bible entries and Generations 6 and 7 from the rent book. It is

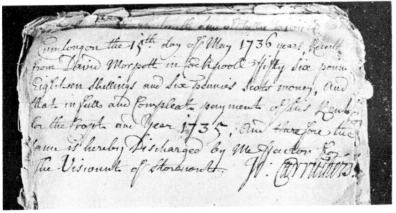

Plate 27. The Morpeth Family Rent Book

interesting that details of births and marriages came not from an original Family Bible but from a copy of the entries sent by Australian cousins. (The original has disappeared.) At the same time, they sent other notes made by a member of the Australian branch during a visit to Scotland in the 1930s. He had interviewed a cousin in her 80s who had provided him not only with the Bible entries but with a fund of family information going back to the early 18th century, another illustration of the value of contacting distant relatives.

A Documentary Biography

Most children will not, of course, have documents as impressive as these. However, at a much simpler level, documents can be used together in order to tell a simple story. For example:

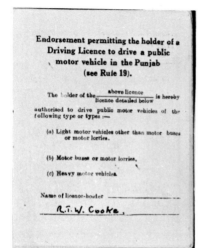 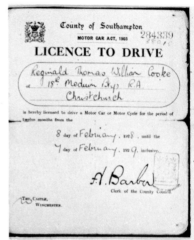

Plates 28-33.

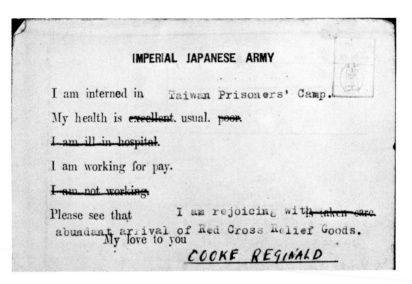

IMPERIAL JAPANESE ARMY

I am interned in ~~Taiwan Prisoners' Camp.~~

My health is ~~excellent~~. usual. ~~poor~~.

~~I am ill in hospital.~~

I am working for pay.

~~I am not working.~~

Please see that I am rejoicing with ~~taken care~~. abundant arrival of Red Cross Relief Goods.
My love to you

COOKE REGINALD

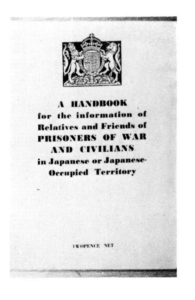

A HANDBOOK
for the information of
Relatives and Friends of
PRISONERS OF WAR
AND CIVILIANS
in Japanese or Japanese-
Occupied Territory

TWOPENCE NET

A Documentary Biography

Plate 34. Every picture tells a story: First generation townsfolk visit Mother, (c.1910)

7 THE PAST IN FOCUS

In the First World War, the camera could record the life of Everyman. It shows the statesmen and generals on parade and off it. It shows the instruments of destruction. Photographs take us into the trenches and munitions factories. We see again the devasted countryside and the queues for food. Here are the men who fought, suffered and died; the human beings behind the ringing phrases. Thanks.to the camera, we can relive the First World War, and not merely read about it.

A.J.P. Taylor, *The First World War: An Illustrated History* (1963), p.9.

THE POTENTIAL of the photograph as a historical record has long been recognised. However, it is only recently that historians like A.J.P. Taylor have seriously considered the usefulness of photographs in sharpening our understanding of a particular event or evoking the atmosphere of an era. More directly applicable to work in the classroom than Taylor's book are those such as O.J. Morris's *Grandfather's London*, a magnificent collection of pictures of London life in the 1880s, and Gordon Winter's *A Country Camera 1844-1914*, in which the pictures are very carefully chosen to make important historical and social statements with a minimum of textual gloss.

The history teacher can use photographs not only to evoke the general atmosphere of a time but also to give personal identity to deceased ancestors and to help children to identify with people, who, though still living, (and indeed talking to the child), are not easily recognisable as the handsome young man or the beautiful young woman portrayed in Grandfather's family album. Listening to Grandad talking about his life, a child is inevitably the spectator rather than the player. Yet even a spectator can become so absorbed in the game that he identifies with his favourite star. As Grandfather talks, the child can be helped to see not the familiar elderly figure facing him, but a boy very much like himself. To make this imaginative leap, he must be provided with visual clues. Thus photographs are almost essential for the success of a Family History project.[1] Moreover, the discussion of them can often act as a conversational catalyst, whereby people and incidents long forgotten are recalled.

Victorian and Edwardian Photographs

Thus children should persuade as many relatives as possible to disinter photographs from the accumulated deposits of years. Most

children are very skilful at doing this, and a surprising number bring
to school Victorian and Edwardian photographs, sometimes in
sumptuous albums. All sorts and conditions of people, except
those of the very humblest station, are represented in these photographs, which are often striking, their formal austere grandeur
conveying much of the atmosphere of their period. As common
as individual portraits are photographs of formal family groups,
with proud parents seated surrounded by their, (usually numerous),
offspring, the boys in sailor suits and the girls in white pinafores. The
most commonly recorded family events are weddings, and if a relative can identify particular individuals for the child, he may be lucky
enough to find he has a photographic *Who's Who* of the entire
family. Group photos of family outings and family games

Plate 35. A photographic *Who's Who* of the entire family

are rarer. (Of course family games tended to be restricted to those
upper class families who had large lawns on which to disport themselves.) The first photographs taken of many rather grubby-looking
back-street urchins may well have been their school photographs,
which again seem to survive in reasonable quantities.

Informal photographs are much rarer. The splendid example
reproduced in Plate 37 would provide the teacher with a great deal
of raw material for discussion or projects, or even for a more formal
lesson on the social history of the period. Of all the photographs,
perhaps the most interesting, but, alas, amongst the rarest, are those
of Victorian and Edwardian interiors, every corner crammed with
bric-a-brac.

Plate 36. Garden party

Plate 37. Edwardian shopkeepers

Family Portraits

A few homes possess not only photographs of ancestors, but portraits or engravings of them. These may date from the 18th century and have been painted by artists who were well-known, at least in their own locality. Even in wealthier homes they became less common once photography was firmly established. Then, large portraits suffered a decline in popularity and miniatures virtually disappeared — the few miniatures so far encountered in Family History projects have all outdated photography.

A form of portraiture which lasted until the colour film became commonly available in the 1950s was the hand-tinted photograph, examples of which can be found in many homes.

More Recent Photographs

Exciting though discovering old photographs often is, one should not assume that these are the only photographs of interest to the Family Historian. The much commoner amateur snapshots of the last 50 years are just as illustrative of social changes and attitudes; the trend-setting drivers of cars and motor-bikes in the 1920s, standing proudly by their well-groomed vehicles, or the voluminous, calf-length skirts of the early 1950s, a reaction against the masculinity and economy of wartime and post-war fashions. The increasing leisure and affluence of the 1960s and early 1970s are reflected in the snapshots of children playing with expensive toys, garden paddling pools or climbing frames, and those of families relaxing outside their chalets and caravans or drinking beer and playing cricket on 'sun-drenched Mediterranean beaches'.

Photo-analysis

Looking with Granny at a pile of photographs is rather like attending a lecture where, despite the disordered profusion of his slides, the speaker holds his audience by his enthusiasm and grasp of detail. Yet, overwhelmed with information, neither child nor audience takes away much more than a confused memory of an enjoyable evening.

Because children grow up in a world in which the visual image is intended to convey an immediately comprehensible message, it is easy to assume a transfer of experience from television commercials and comics to more sophisticated forms of visual communication. However, although the present generation in our schools is more used to the visual media, the understanding and appreciation of visual images requires just as much training as does concept formation. As Strong has pointed out, 'We must not assume with reference to pictures, any more than in the case of time-charts and maps, that children will comprehend them by the light of nature'.[2] Massaged by the medium, they miss the meaning of the message. If used as historical evidence, photographs require individual analysis, comparison with others and oral or documentary corroboration.

Primary Children

When looking at a photograph, younger children can think about the following points:

1. Who or what is shown on the photo-graph? Is anything written on the back which will help? Can any of your relatives tell you?

2. If you know who or what is in the picture, does it help you to learn more about what you have already found out from talking to people?

3. If no one can tell you any more about the picture, what clues are in it which might help you to say who or what is shown and when the picture was taken? For, example, can you find out when people wore the sort of clothes shown in the photograph, or when any of the objects shown in it were being used?

Plate 38. The photographer's name and address may be an aid to identification

Considering such questions may en-able even Primary children to give a photograph an approximate date. The teacher may help by mounting a series of photographs and asking them to identify each picture as accurately as possible from the reference books available in the classroom.

Secondary Pupils

Older children will be able to engage in more sophisticated forms of analysis and verification, dating photographs by recognising the style of studio backdrop or the photographic process used.

Backdrops

As children are used to their parents (and in many cases them-selves) taking outdoor snaps, it may not occur to them that in Victorian and Edwardian times very few people could afford cameras, and that the vast majority of photographs were taken by professional photographers, either in their studios, or in their subjects' own homes. Thus, whereas the teacher will recognise a painted balustrade and a cardboard swan (Plate 39), a child may see what he would expect to be there — a real balustrade and a real swan like those in the snap taken of him on a visit to Hampton Court. However, as with Tudor and mock-Tudor architecture, the child can be taught to discriminate. Once he has realised that the studio backdrops were a highly stylised convention and not intended to deceive, and that, as with clothes, their fashions changed, he can use them to date a Victorian picture with a fair degree of accuracy: in the 1860s the fashionable backdrop was balustrade, column and curtain; in the 1870s, rustic bridge and stile; in the 1880s, hammock, swing and railway carriage; in the 1890s, palm trees, cockatoos and bicycles; in the early 20th century, motor-cycles and side-cars.[3]

Plate 39.
Swan & Steps (1870's)
Painted backcloth and 'water'
and cardboard swan are expertly
combined with a real rock and fence

Plate 40.
Rustic Glade (1870's)
Here the backdrop is realistic but
a second-rate cairn gives the
game away

Early Photographic Processes

It was Louis Jacques Mande Daguerre (1789-1851), the stage designer and inventor of the Diorama, who managed to develop a photographic image from an exposure in a camera, in a much shorter time than had previously been thought possible. Taken on a polished silvered copper plate, sensitised with iodine vapour, the exposure at first took up to 30 minutes, making portraiture almost impossible until further improvements were made in the early 1840s, reducing the exposure time to about six seconds. This problem once solved, the *Daguerreotype* enjoyed a boom for over a decade. Although it was expensive (£2.50 for a quarter plate portrait) thousands were produced from 1840 onwards. However, very few originals have survived. Distinguishable by the clear rendering and detail on the picture, Daguerrotypes are, in the words of John Pudney, 'totally distinctive from any other kind of picture, and once seen can never be again mistaken'.[4]

The *Talbotype* or *Calotype* process of negative/positive photography on paper was first developed in 1841, by W.H. Fox Talbot, a Wiltshire squire. The Calotype was popular until the early 1850s because of its cheapness and adaptibility — it could be multiplied indefinitely, whereas the Daguerrotype photograph could not. However, the Calotype suffered from several disadvantages: a portrait exposure took six or more minutes in bright sunlight, the purplish brown mezzotint and soft graining of the paper was generally considered to compare unfavourably with the exquisitely delicate brilliance of the Daguerrotype, and above all, the Calotype faded quickly. From about 1848 both it and the Daguerrotype were overshadowed by the *Ambrotype*, originated by Frederick Scott Archer.

Plates 41 and 42. Ambrotypes (1860s)

Archer's process which was much cheaper than either of the others, became even more popular after 1850, when Blanquart-Evrard introduced the use of albumen positive paper. The glossy surface of the printed-out picture was usually toned with chloride of gold to improve its colour and permanence. These photographs remained popular until the early 1880s.

In 1871 the microscopist, Dr. Richard Leach-Maddox, showed the feasibility of using a gelatine dry plate, instead of the wet collodion plate used by Archer. By 1878 the gelatine plate was being factory-produced on a large scale. It could be stored for a long period and enabled near instantaneous photographs to be taken. The familiar celluloid film dates from the late 1880s, and by the early 1900s the Eastman Company's nitro-cellulose roll film accounted for 80-90% of the total world output. The non-inflammable cellulose acetate film now used dates from the 1930s.

Dating by backdrops or processes should be used in conjunction with other methods of identification as shown in the following flow-chart.

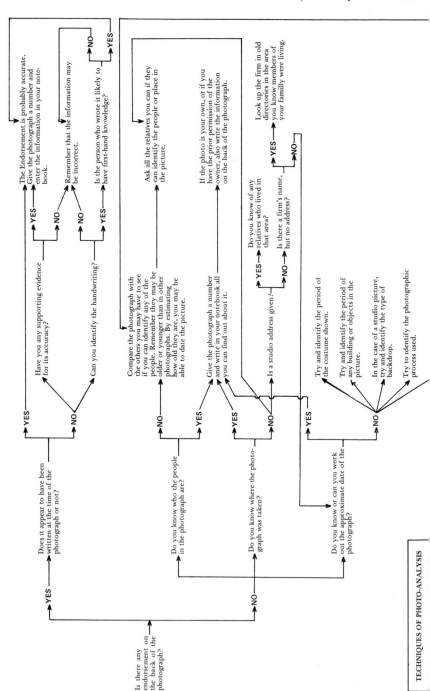

TECHNIQUES OF PHOTO-ANALYSIS

Photo Assemblage

Valuable though the single photograph may be in helping us to visualise a person or place in the past, like documents, photographs are even more valuable when used in groups.

Photo-series

Here, several photographs are used to tell a simple story of people, places or things, or to assist the development of time concepts by relating time to the ageing process.[5] The series may form a pictorial biography or a Family History (see inside front cover). It may depict successive changes in costume, transport, or housing, though here there is a danger that over-concentration on things may leave out people.

Although, traditionally, one moves chronologically forwards in telling a story, there is no reason why a series of photographs should not be used in reverse order, to provide stepping stones linking the child with the past.

Unlike the conditioned adult, young children may well find moving backwards as logical as moving forwards. Indeed, they may perhaps find it easier to move back step by step to Grandad as a boy, than to make a flash-back and then come forwards, a mental practice which the adult with years of memories behind him performs automatically.

Photo-synthesis

Although a photo-series may be very effective in helping children to conceptualize spans of time of up to 70 or 80 years (or even longer if earlier generations are incorporated into the story), in historical terms, it is impoverished through lack of the corroboration provided by oral, documentary or archaeological evidence. The simplest way of remedying this, is to use a mixture of documents and pictures. Inside the cover a single document is used as a focus for a group of pictures. Equally, one photograph could be used as the focus for a group of documents. Overleaf several of each have been put together to tell a story. It is interesting to compare this one with the Second World War P.O.W. story (pp.82-83) told entirely through documents. Most would agree that the latter would have become more personal had photographs been included.

Photographs can be used in conjunction with oral evidence by accompanying a display with a tape-recorded commentary incorporating relevant extracts from people's memories. The use of photographs and artefacts in conjunction is discussed in chapter 9.

Photo-antithesis

This has long been used by teachers to make vivid contrasts e.g. past and present, town and country, different social classes. Photographs may be mounted in pairs, in contrasting groups, or even in two contrasting complete wall displays.

Plate 44. In Training

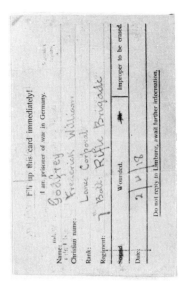

Plates 45 and 46. Captured but Safe

Plate 43. Enlisted

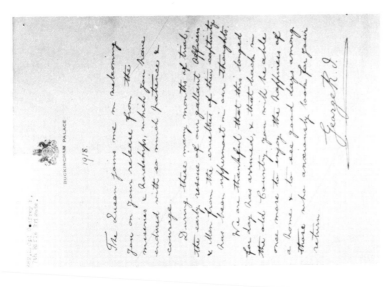

Plate 49. A Letter from the King

Plates 47 and 48. A Prison Camp
somewhere in Germany

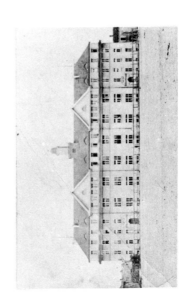

The Archive Code: Photographs

Children should be encouraged not only to try and date the family photographs, but to document today's photographs as they are taken. Each new print should have written on the back the date when it was taken, by whom, where, plus a key to any persons portrayed. One way of doing this effectively is to trace very lightly the outline of figures in the photograph, adding their names and other details. This can be then stuck on the back as a permanent record. Apart from the value of this work to a future historian of the family, it is excellent training in the precise and accurate recording and documentation of evidence.

Notes and References

1   As was shown in the B.B.C. documentary *Two Victorian Girls* (1969. Re-shown 1971), the same objective can be achieved more effectively with cine-film when aged features melt into youthful ones or *vice versa*. An even more imaginative use of cinematographic techniques is the animation of what purports to be a still period photograph, the whole scene springing suddenly to life, a technique used by John Gibson in *Tommy Steele in Search of Charlie Chaplin* (B.B.C., 1971).

2   C.F. Strong, *History in the Secondary School* (1958), p.119.

3   Helmut and Alison Gernsheim, *Concise History of Photography* (1965), p.121.

4   O.J. Morris, *Grandfather's London* (1956), Preface, p.9.

5   This theme is developed further in *Family History in Schools 2: The Main-Line Programme*.

8 YESTERDAY'S NEWS

> Newspapers have . . . from the beginning been a mirror of social
> life and customs . . . The newspaper reflects the spirit of its age
> and helps to create the spirit of tomorrow.
>
> E.A. Smith, *A History of the Press*(1970), p.6.

USING NEWSPAPERS to teach history is hardly original. What is
rarely emphasised is that the children themselves may often be able
to provide the papers, and, indeed many families may not realise
they possess such treasures until they investigate the grubby
wrapping-paper around long-stored articles in Granny's attic, the
lining-paper of cupboards and shelves and the bottoms of long-
undisturbed trunks and drawers. In places such as these even a
modern 'semi' may have preserved newspapers up to 10 years old.
One home produced a large drawer full of papers from 1900 to the
present day. A few of these had been kept because they contained
references to members of the family. Many more concerned royal
births, weddings, funerals and coronations. Others celebrated the
victories of 1918 and 1945.

Browsing among these back numbers it was particularly interesting to find a copy of the *British Gazette* of Tuesday 11 May 1926,
produced during the General Strike and headed in thick black type,
'Please pass on this copy or display it'. It contained a leader by the
Attorney-General, Sir Douglas Hogg (later Lord Hailsham), the
father of Quintin Hogg, rejecting any suggestion that the Government was to blame for the strike. Amid the news on the front page
was a short account of Lieut. Byrd's successful flight over the
North Pole.

The crippling effect of the strike on the newspaper industry was
illustrated by a copy of the *Evening News* for the fourth day of the
strike. It consisted of two duplicated foolscap sheets. There was
also a copy of the *N.C.U. Bulletin* 'published for the general good',
by the National Citizens' Union. The collection also contained
copies of *The British Worker*, the official strike news-bulletin published by the General Council of the Trades Union Congress. Its
headlines included: 'Every Docker Out' and 'South Wales is Solid'.

The earliest item in this remarkable collection consisted
of pages 7 and 8 of the *Daily Graphic* for 18 January 1900.
Page 8 was almost completely taken up with a sketch by an officer
of the British 'check' (i.e. defeat) at Colenso on 15 December.
Alongside was a report of the battle, which contained the poignant
'We had to attack an invisible enemy, whose position could not
even be fixed by the smoke of his rifles'. An alert pupil might

wonder why, so long after the invention of the electric telegraph, the report of the battle was appearing over a month after the event, and even the teacher might hesitate for an answer![1]

Page 7 reported that the bishops had agreed to recommend to the clergy that Septuagesima Sunday should be generally observed as a day of special intercession for the nation and the troops, in connection with the war in South Africa.

The plays performed at the London theatres on the same day included *Two Little Vagabonds, A Pretty Piece of Business, A Bad Penny, The Gay Lord Quex, The Bugle Call, A Greek Slave, Jerry and a Sunbeam* and *A Pair of Knickerbockers*. To be fair, you could also have gone to see *A Midsummer Night's Dream, She Stoops to Conquer* or *David Garrick*.

The *News of the World* for 10 August 1902, which reports the Coronation of Edward VII, is equally fascinating. It includes such choice items, as, 'Motor Car Runs Amok — Nine Persons injured at Wandsworth'. There are intriguing descriptions of court cases, such as 'Charge of Child Stealing — Remarkable Conduct of a Professional Beggar'. An interesting feature is the column devoted to medical and legal advice; for example, a collier of Nantyglo, who had lost a limb, is advised, 'You cannot do anything better than bathing the stump in cold water with Tidman's Sea Salt dissolved in it, and also rub in some whiskey into the tender skin'. 'Bertha' is informed, 'The only way in which your brother can compel his daughters to maintain him is by going in the workhouse. The Guardians will then take the necessary steps, if the daughters have any means'. One suspects that in the former case the whiskey might not be used for rubbing, and the latter advice was unlikely to be acceptable, unless the workhouse was as inviting as that in Plate 50.

Thus the news stories and correspondence columns evoke the atmosphere and give insight into social problems such as drink, poverty, unemployment, crime and poor housing, as well as more cheerful aspects of the past. For older children, the newspaper editorials and the tone of news reporting will provide clues as to the political allegiance of the

TUESDAY, JANUARY 20, 1920.

COSY FLAT IN THE WORKHOUSE.

Vision of Hills and Fields From the Window.

"It will be like living in a West End flat," said the Master of the Barnet Workhouse yesterday when he showed a " Daily News " representative over the three-roomed home which was being fitted up for the benefit of Mr. William Oliver, a disabled ex-soldier, of Finchley.

The Oliver family, as explained in " The Daily News " on Saturday, have been unable to find a house, and the Barnet Guardians have agreed to take them as paying guests at 10s. a week.

Plate 50. 'Oliver', 1920 version

paper, what issues preoccupied people's minds, and what at least one section of the public thought about them.

Advertisements

The advertisements can provide a great deal of information which is quite incidental to the advertiser's intention. For example, advertisements for soap may provide good illustrations of the homes and clothes of working class people (see Plate 51). All kinds of

51. Sunlit home, *The Graphic*, 1889

commodities are portrayed, as well as their prices. Whereas Great-grandmother's memory may well confuse the dates when various prices were current, a newspaper can date prices to the day. Besides this, children can easily discover details about house prices, rentals, the range of shops, wage-rates and job-opportunities for both men and women, transport (timetables, fares) and entertainments. They can also assess the claims of the patent-medicine salesmen, although not all were as bold as the advertiser in the 1902 *News of the World* who claimed his medicine 'cures every known ailment'. Children can compare these with their modern equivalents.

Newspaper Cuttings

Although not all families will have old newspapers, most will have kept newspaper cuttings, particularly of births, marriages and deaths, as well as items concerning the sporting, dramatic or musical activities of members of the family.

A particularly interesting type of newspaper cutting is the report of an incident that took place long before. Here is a mid-19th century event reported in a New Zealand paper in 1933, a cutting of which was sent to an English relative. Henry Douglas Morpeth and his family (see page 70) emigrated from Scotland to Prince Edward Island off the coast of Nova Scotia, but, becoming disillusioned with Canada, he persuaded his friends and neighbours to join him in re-emigrating from Canada to New Zealand in 1859.

> The recent death in Auckland of Lady Parr has brought to mind . . . the voyage of the brig Prince Edward from Prince Edward Island to Auckland in 1859 with close upon 100 immigrants. Lady Parr was a daughter of the late Mr. W.C. Haszard, one of the passengers.
>
> The venture was promoted by members of two families, the Morpeths, and the Haszards, living in and near Charlotte Town, Prince Edward Island. According to Mr. Sydney Haszard, it was not inspired by the earlier Nova Scotian expedition, but by a book, 'New Zealand or Zealandia, the Britain of the South', which had been published in London by Charles Hursthouse, a former resident of Taranaki, in the year 1857.
>
> A Prosperous Voyage
>
> To the people in Charlotte Town, who enjoyed a summer climate for only four months of the year, the land pictured in the book seemed much like an earthly paradise. Two of their number H.D. Morpeth and Robert Haszard, built a stout brig of 174 tons register, and seven months after she had left the stocks they set sail in her with their own and a number of other families, totalling altogether some 95 men, women and children. The captain whom they had engaged also had his wife and four children with him, The cargo, in addition to luggage, included furniture, agricultural implements, house fittings and some steam machinery.

The little vessel must have been very crowded, but passengers and crew came of a hardy race, and the long voyage of over five months passed without a single casualty — an uncommon record in those days. Perhaps the presence of a doctor on board had something to do with it. An account printed in the Auckland newspaper, the *New Zealander*, of May 14, 1859, offers a strong contrast with sea travel of today.

> The long-looked-for brig Prince Edward, Captain Nowlan, arrived in harbour on Thursday night, from Prince Edward Island, after a protracted passage of 162 days. She sailed from Charlotte Town on the 1st and cleared the coast on the 4th December. She caught the North East Trade in 28 deg. North latitude; but they were very indifferent and the South East Trade, though good, hung very far to the North. Crossed the equator on the 1st January, in longtitude 31 deg. West, and put into Pernambuco on the 9th, remaining there five days.
>
> Experienced a series of calms in the horse latitudes; and went into Simon's Bay, Cape of Good Hope, on the 17th February, resting there the next four-and-twenty days to refresh. There were the Boscawen line of battleship, 70 guns, and five other English men-of-war in Simon's Bay, from whence four sail of Russian cruisers had but a short time previously taken their departure.
>
> From the Cape to Van Diemen's Land the passage was made in the short space of 31 days. Captain Nowlan running down his Easting between the parallels of 40 degrees and 43 degrees south

latitude, carrying strong winds, and passing to the Southward of Tasmania, in a dense fog, and with a heavy gale. From thence to the Three Kings, which was sighted on the 4th instant. The distance was performed in seven days, the vessel clearing ninety degrees longitude in eighteen days.

In all, this remarkable voyage covered 14,000 miles.

Newspapers in Your Local Library

The old newspapers brought in by the children can often be supplemented by extracts from the files of local or national newspapers at a public library. From this almost inexhaustible supply of material, papers can be photocopied in small sections, pieced together and stuck on card. Where the library is controlled by the same local authority as the school, it will often be prepared to charge at cost rather than the full commercial rate of 5p per photocopy. About nine copies will be needed to reproduce one large sheet, so at commercial rates it would cost about £2.00 to reproduce four pages. However, this is a non-recurring item of expenditure as the reproductions can be preserved by being stuck onto card and protected by a transparent, tackyback sheet.

Many local libraries will have collections of newspapers going back to the 18th century. (Newspapers have been published in London since the mid-17th century, but did not appear in the provinces until 1701). In general, news of purely local, rather than national interest did not appear until the latter half of the 18th century, though there were often local advertisements much earlier.

Perhaps the most interesting, if sinister entries in local newspapers are the detailed accounts of trials which are every bit as sensational as the reports in the modern popular press.

Here is an account from the *Herts Mercury* for Saturday 10 March 1827, referring to a distant relative of one of the authors.

Elisha Kitchener, (an Old offender) was charged with feloniously breaking and entering a wheel house, part of the dwelling house of Edward Nevens of Tring and stealing therefrom two copper boilers, a fishing net, a pair of boots etc., his property.

Mr. Jessopp conducted the prosecution.

Oxley Seabrook examined. — I am servant to Edward Nevens, the Prosecutor. He lives at Tring, in this County, I remember fastening master's wheel house door the night of the robbery. It contained a fishnet and a pair of boots. I got up at six the next morning and found the door of the wheelhouse off the hinges. I missed the articles mentioned in the indictment. My master also lost five geese.

William Seabrook sworn. Is servant to Mr. Nevens. In November last he got up about six o'clock and discovered the robbery.

Thomas Dean examined. I am a shoemaker at Albury about 2 miles and a half from Tring. I know the prisoner at the Bar. I saw him on Saturday evening, the 18th November at the Valiant Trooper Public House. He asked me if I wanted to buy a goose or two, as he had got five. I answered, 'Perhaps they are stale'. He

said 'No, they are not, as Matthew and I fetched them last night'.
By Matthew he meant Matthew Sharp.

George Thorn sworn — I live at Albury. I was at the public
house with the prisoner and Dean. Prisoner called me out of the
house and said he had five fat geese, 2 copper boilers, a fish net,
a pair of boot tops, a gridiron and a band saw which were worth
altogether six or seven pounds and that he would sell them all. He
said they were under lock and key at Wilmer's house and that the
geese were hid in the ground in a wood.

Edward Nevens, the Prosecutor, examined. I live at Tring. On
17th November last I saw the property which was stolen safe in
the wheelhouse. On that evening it was stolen. In consequence of
information I received from the last witness I went to Wilmer's
home where I found the two boilers, the boots and the boot
tops and the net. The prisoner ran away that night but was
apprehended on 12th December. I took him to Mr. Lacey,
the Magistrate. He there confessed the robbery which he said was
committed by him, Matthew Sharp and William Wilmer. No
promise or threat was held out to him. He said the goose they
buried in Turnhanger Wood and when they went to fetch them
they were gone. The wheelhouse is part of my dwelling house.
The property stolen was worth more than 40 shillings.

The Jury returned a verdict of GUILTY — DEATH recorded.

Fascinating though such newspaper accounts are, only a very
determined and fortunate pupil will be able to find a report
concerning an ancestor or relative, unless he had some claim to
fame. However, if pupils have traced ancestors in the locality back
to the early 19th century or before, newspapers will provide them
with invaluable background information. As with any other source,
however, it is important that they should be used in conjunction
with other primary and secondary sources, or significant points will
be missed. Thus Elisha's shortcomings can perhaps be viewed more
sympathetically in the light of what William Cobbett had to say
about Tring when he visited it two years later. Commenting
bitterly that 'the labouring people are suffering in a degree not to
be described', he foresaw that unless such grinding poverty was
alleviated, the poor, their patience exhausted, would band together
to raid and loot the well-stocked pantries and cellars of their
masters.[2] His prediction that this would develop into widespread
rioting by mobs of labourers was realised a few months later,
though strangely enough not in Tring and hardly at all in
Hertfordshire.[3] Of course, it can be argued that Cobbett was not
so much observing the rural scene as actually inciting the labourers
to fulfil his own prophesies.[4] Be that as it may, it would be a
very perceptive pupil who would realise from the newspaper alone
that he was looking at the period only from the point of view of the
propertied classes.

Reprints

Many newspaper companies have reprinted back numbers for

one reason or another — often an important anniversary. However, it is only recently that the commercial possibilities of reprinting have been fully appreciated. In 1970, David and Charles produced the bound volume *Newspapers of the First World War*, and in 1972, Peter Way Ltd. started a regular monthly series of *Great Newspapers Reprinted.*[5] Extremely important also is the bi-monthly magazine *Then*, directed by Professor Asa Briggs. Each issue is a collection of newspaper and magazine extracts for a single year.[6] Clearly, these reprints are extremely useful for Family History work.

Magazines

National Weeklies

The commonest are *Picture Post* and *Illustrated*, particularly those for the war years. Others include *Everybody's* and *John Bull*, as well as the more expensive *Illustrated London News*. Occasionally children will be given runs of Victorian or Edwardian magazines, particularly *Punch*. An interesting, but less usual example is the fine run of *Black and White* covering the whole of the Boer War, a few copies of which are shown in Plate 53.

Parish Magazines

Parish Magazines are perhaps more useful in a Local History project than a Family History one. However, though at first sight rather unpromising, they can furnish many clues on social history, good works and moral and religious attitudes. For example, a cursory glance at the *St. Barnabas and St. Silas, South Kennington Parish Magazine* for November 1913, might overlook the two advertisements for Licensed Cowkeepers operating in Inner London. An article proposes the establishment of co-operative kitchens for the poor in order to reduce the cost of foodstuffs by bulk buying; they would also 'serve as a training ground for girls going out to service as kitchen or scullery maids'. Another article begins: 'Possibly

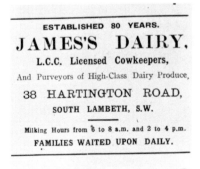

Plate 52.
Cows in Lambeth

Plate 53.
Black and White in South Africa

in the midst of the world's wild rush after what it conceives to be novel or original . . .' *Mutatis mutandis!* One of the Vicar's 'Red Letter Church News' flashes was:

> At a fire which destroyed five stacks at Berden Hall, Essex, the Vicar of Berden, the Rev. H.K. Hudom, dragged a fire engine, which he had made himself, to the spot, his wife assisting with the hose truck, and rendered good service until the arrival of a steam fire-engine.

Sports and Hobbies Journals

These exist in greater profusion in this country than in almost any other in the world. Many like the *Pigeon Fancier* or *Angler* will not perhaps be of much help in a Family History project, except as illustrations of personal interests. Occasionally, however, copies have been kept because they record exploits of a member of the family.

Other Magazines

Nearly all occupations, trade unions, regiments, clubs and societies produce their own magazines, and sometimes have been doing so for more than a century. Like the parish magazines, these can often give fascinating glimpses of the past.

Catalogues

Another source which social historians have recently recognised as extremely useful is old catalogues. *Yesterday's Shopping*, the Army and Navy Stores Catalgoue for 1907, reproduced by David & Charles (1969) is very useful but expensive, and teachers may prefer to approach old-established local firms to see if they are willing either to give or to lend an old catalogue to the school. In Dudley, teachers under the direction of their local inspector, John West, have photocopied a great deal of this type of material for their local Resources Centre.[7]

Directories

Where children's families are of relatively local origin, pupils can use trade directories to try to trace them. The most comprehensive for the early 19th century are Piggott's, White's, Kelly's and the Post Office London Directory. Such old directories will often be found in the reference sections of local libraries. There is a magnificent collection of London directories in the Guildhall Library. Several mid-19th century directories have been reprinted,[8] most include much useful background information on places.

Apart from locating the homes of their ancestors, children may also use these directories to try to find the photographers whose names appear on unendorsed photographs.

Children's Literature

Children's magazines and comics reflect not only children's interests, but also the relationships between children and adults, technological developments and the general preoccupations of the time. The changing scene in entertainment for example may be encapsulated in the titles of popular comics like *Radio Fun,* or *Film Fun.*

It is likely that the children will bring to school a number of Victorian and Edwardian anthologies, such as *The Child's Companion* of 1902, perhaps given to the grandparents and great-grandparents as presents or prizes. Although many of the stories will strike children to day as 'pious', they do, in fact, provide excellent material for involving children in discussions on the attitudes and opinions of the day. The emphasis on religion and morally improving tales, the ardent patriotism and belief in our Imperial mission, as well as the articles extolling the virtue of members of the Royal Family, will contrast sharply with contemporary ideals. Younger pupils may be more interested in the pictures of toys and children playing. Again, the advertisements are a source of interesting comparisons with the present and the illustrations will provide useful guides to costume, especially that worn by children.

Wartime Miscellanea

The complexity of Second World War regulations and controls necessitated personal documents such as identity cards and ration books. There was also a flood of exhortatory pamphlets such as *Your Food in Wartime, Your Gas Mask; How to Keep it and how to use it*, designed both to give essential information and to sustain public morale. Perhaps the most useful of these for Family History purposes is the Government's *War Emergency Information and Instructions*, which includes information about areas scheduled for evacuation as well as instructions for the evacuees. It ends with the following optimistic advice in block capitals: DO NOT TAKE TOO MUCH NOTICE OF NOISE IN AN AIR-RAID. MUCH OF IT WILL BE THE NOISE OF OUR OWN GUNS DEALING WITH THE RAIDERS. KEEP A GOOD HEART! WE ARE GOING TO WIN THROUGH.

Printed Ephemera

Apart from war pamphlets, the most common ephemera are: membership cards and other literature produced for all kinds of recreational clubs, learned societies, religious bodies and political organisations; invitations to parties, dances and presentations, menus, theatre, cinema, concert or sporting programmes, catalogues of auctions and exhibitions, holiday brochures, guide-books and maps.

Such ephemera are often ignored by parents and children as of
no family significance. However, many of them will provide
interesting clues as to ancestors' biographical details and interests,
and in some cases they can be useful indicators as to where further
information about an ancestor might be found.

The Archive Code: Newspapers and Magazines

Archive consciousness can be aroused by asking the children
to preserve at the time, newspapers and magazines dealing with
events which future generations are likely to recognise as significant,
such as the assassination of President Kennedy, the Arab-Israeli
War, Chichester's around-the-World voyage, the invasion of
Czechoslovakia, the First Moon landing, the First Heart Transplant,
Jumbo Jets, Colour Television and Decimalization. In this way
children can not only preserve a record of these events for their
own grandchildren, but can employ with regard to current events
some of the criteria they use in assessing the importance of historical
events. Trees should be planted as well as felled: the events of
today will be history in the classrooms of tomorrow.

Notes and References

1. A report did in fact appear earlier, but the sketch had to be sent over-
    land and by sea. Hence the delay. A second report was included to
    arouse interest in the sketch.

2. William Cobbett, *Rural Rides* (Everyman edn., 1912), Vol. ii, p.215.

3. E.J. Hobsbawm and G. Rude, *Captain Swing* (1969), p.305.

4. *Ibid.*, p.104.

5. These have included *The Golden Daily Mail* (1901), *The Daily Express*
    (World War II, 1939), *The Times* (Charge of the Light Brigade, 1854),
    The Daily Mirror (Abdication of Edward VIII, 1936), *The Daily
    Graphic* (Bleriot flies the Channel, 1909) and a selection of General
    Strike newspapers (1926). Copies may be obtained from Peter Way Ltd.,
    28 James Street, Covent Garden, London W.C.2E 8PA.

6. The first issue was devoted to 1901. Copies may be obtained from The
    Proprietors of Then Ltd., 28 James St., Covent Garden, London W.C.2E
    8PA.

7. See John West, 'The Development of a Local Resources Centre',
    Teaching History, Vol. 2, no. 7 (May 1972), pp.228-235.

8. David & Charles have reprinted the following old directories: *Three
    Victorian Telephone Directories*; *White's* directories of *Norfolk* (1856);
    Suffolk (1844); *Leeds and the Clothing Districts of Yorkshire* (1853);
    Devon (1850).

9 CLASSROOM COLLECTOMANIA

Schools can build up their own simple collection; a pair of candle snuffers turned out of a cupboard, a faded letter in copybook hand . . . these can so easily become talismans to conjure up the past.

Ministry of Education Pamphlet No. 23, *Teaching History* (1952), p.25.

ARTEFACTS SURVIVING from the past are one of the most important historical sources we can use with children. An object one can handle, clothes one can wear, are more meaningful than the best pictures in books. In the course of a Family History project children should therefore be encouraged to bring to school not only documents and other printed material, but any other objects they think may be relevant to their study. Dad may have an old watch, inherited from his grandfather, Great Aunt Emily a Victorian doll which used to belong to her grandmother; Uncle Harry a walking stick that has 'always been in the family'; a second cousin a flint-lock which, tradition has it, was used by an ancestor at Waterloo. The very age of such heirlooms gives them irresistible fascination, while the fact that such treasures were used by members of their own families reinforces their interest with a sense of personal involvement.

In all schools which have engaged in Family History projects, the pupils have brought in many interesting souvenirs, and it was found that these could be most useful to the projects if, instead of just being shown to the class and then taken home again at the end of the day, they were arranged to form displays in a classroom museum.

Although such a museum will rarely contain any object of great monetary value, it has certain advantages over a public collection: it is assembled by the children who have a personal interest in the objects; they have it constantly at their disposal and can look at it in spare moments; items from the collection can be picked up, passed round and examined — clothes and jewellery may even be worn; and as most objects are only on temporary loan the collect-tion is a live one, and not a permanent and dusty fixture.

The organisation of such a museum of course needs careful plan-ning so as to ensure that the best use may be made of all available material. Relatives will lend objects more readily if they are not only asked, verbally, by the child, but also sent a duplicated letter. It may be wise to add a tear-off slip to the letter and ask for this to be returned before the loan is brought to school, so that one knows in advance what objects one may expect, and can decide what kinds of displays to mount. Each child should be given a number of letters for distribution to relatives and friends, rather than just one for parents.

Dear Sir/Madam,

As you are probably aware, Class 4 is engaged in a Family History Project in which the children are studying the history of the last century or so, through what happened to their own families in this period. Associated with the project a classroom museum has been set up. If you have anything which you think may be of interest to the children, which you are prepared to lend for a limited period, I would be most grateful if you would kindly complete the attached slip. The greatest care will, of course, be taken of any objects on loan.

Yours sincerely

Child's Name .... *Class* ....

Name of lender .... *Address* ....

....

Telephone No. ....
Please tick where appropriate

I would be prepared to lend:-

Old domestic utensils – e.g. old flat irons; butter pats.
Small portraits, photographs and postcards.
Documents – e.g. old letters, diaries.
Campaign medals and War souvenirs e.g. gas-mask, ration-books, pamphlets.
Toys, dolls and games (pre-1939).
Newspapers or magazines more than ten years old.
Children's books (pre-1939).
Old School text books and exercise books.
Clothes (pre-1945) including war uniforms, arm bands, helmets.
Embroidery – particularly Victorian samplers, antimaccassars.
Ornaments – musical boxes, vases, Victorian seaside pottery, novelties.
Souvenir mugs e.g. Coronations.
Objects connected with occupations, e.g. miner's lamp, policeman's truncheon, railway guard's whistle, craftsman's tools.
Old Rent books and Insurance cards.
Any.other objects which you think might be of interest. Please specify.

....

Specimen letter to parents, relatives and friends

In one primary school,[1] two classes of seven- and eight-year-olds brought the following items to school: a hospital tag for a new born baby; birth certificates; baby clothes (including a christening dress); games, toys and books used by their parents as children; a silver spoon; Ration Books and Identity Cards; gas masks; an R.A.F. cap dating from 1945; a variety of medals dating from 1908 (Italian) to the present day; various old coins; cups and certificates for sports, hobbies and examinations; contemporary magazines from both wars; old newspapers and newspaper cuttings; mugs and plates; a wedding spoon; wedding anniversary cards; numerous old photographs; family Bibles.

Relatives are prepared to trust older children with much more. At one secondary school[2] first-formers brought in well over 500 items in the course of a single term — enough material for several different displays. When items are returned to anyone other than the immediate family, the child responsible for the loan should write a short letter of thanks.

Plate 54. The Classroom Museum: St. Cuthbert's Junior School, Wigan

Types of Display

There is a real danger that the classroom will rapidly become submerged under a sea of bric-a-brac. For this reason, the forms should be returned to the teacher without the objects, so that the amount of material available can be assessed. The teacher can then decide what kind of display to put on.

Generational

Here the display is a general one but limited to the particular generation studied at the time.

Plate 55. Generational display

Thematic

A display on a particular theme. This may be restricted to one period (e.g. The Home Front during the Second World War), or may extend over several generations (e.g. Lighting and Heating in Generations 1-5).

Plate 56. Thematic display

Plate 57. The Apothecary's Shop
(St. Cuthbert's Junior School, Wigan)

Plate 57. 1815 Dress and
Underwear
(St. Cuthbert's)

Plate 59. Washing Day
50 Years Ago
(St. Cuthbert's)

Thematic displays can be particularly useful for demonstrating social change, and it is worth remembering that objects need not be very old to be of historical interest. Thus many primary children have never seen any kind of pen other than the ball-point variety. Children enjoy using in succession a quill (first recorded in the 7th century), a steel-nibbed pen (invented c.1825), a fountain pen (invented c.1880) and a ball-point (invented c.1935).[1]

Focal

Here an exhibition is built around a single item (e.g. a miner's lamp or a Victorian doll). This becomes the focus for related objects and other illustrative material. Wherever possible, such displays should be arranged so as to set the objects in a context of appropriate photographs or documents. Plate 60, for example, shows six swimming medals won in 1900 by the grandmother of a girl at Maiden Erlegh School. These become much more meaningful when set beside a photograph of the 14-year-old champion and a selection of the certificates awarded to her. Even a little display

Plate 60. Swimming Medals, 1900

like this can provoke a number of interesting questions:

> Which swimming baths in Reading did people use? How much did it cost to get in? What sort of swimming costumes did people wear? Has Grandma any photos of herself in a costume? Did they teach swimming in schools? Did they have women's swimming in the Olympic Games? What other sports were there for women?

Questions such as these can lead not only to further information being obtained from Grandma, but can be used by the teacher to raise larger issues such as women's role in Society at that time.

Plates 61-63. Photographs and Documents will provide objects with a context

Display Cases

Both teachers and parents are sensibly wary of allowing objects of monetary or sentimental value to be brought to school. Problems of security are particularly difficult in secondary schools, where the room containing a classroom museum may be used by eight different teachers and classes in the course of one day. For this reason it is a good idea to put objects of possible value in a perspex or glass-fronted case. Disembowelled television sets and bakers' cake display units can by very successfully adapted for this purpose, but if the co-operation of a woodwork master can be secured, pupils may be able to make their own cases with sliding perspex fronts. Obviously these will not deter a thief, but they will protect objects from damage and pilfering.[4]

Museum Cards

It is a good general principle to ask any child who brings an object for the museum briefly to describe it, tell how he came by it and explain its function. The pupil should also make a display card for his loan. These should be very specific. For example:

OBJECT	*The bowl of a clay pipe with a broken piece of stem.*
BROUGHT BY	*John Thompson, Form 3a.*
OWNER	*Mr. James Miller, 7 Foxglove Lane (John's Uncle).*
WHERE AND WHEN FOUND	*At Mr. Miller's cottage in the summer of 1965. It was discovered behind the hearth by workmen who were modernising the cottage.*
APPROX. DATE	*Between 1750 and 1800. See the pictures of clay pipes in Wood's* Field Guide to Archaeology, *pp.279-280.*
ANY FURTHER INFORMATION	*These pipes were known as Churchwardens' pipes because they were smoked a lot by Churchwardens. The bowl is very small because tobacco cost a lot of money and Churchwardens could not afford much.*

Once a collection of such cards has been made it provides a 'bank' which easily can be drawn upon during future project work. Younger children can make such cards so long as they are asked very specific questions about the object. The questions asked about the clay pipe were:

> What is it? Who smoked this kind of pipe? How long ago do you think they were used? Why were they made of clay? Why is the bowl so small? Where did the tobacco come from?

A group of 10-year-olds enjoys answering such questions.

We have found that 8 in. x 6 in. is the most convenient size for record cards as children often discover a lot of information and their handwriting tends to be big.

Log-Book

Although in theory the record card system provides a check on all items brought for display, in practice, cards can be lost. A log book should therefore be kept as well, either by the teacher or, on a rota basis, by children given the imposing title of *Museum Curator*.

Museum's Schools' Services

A teacher building a classroom museum should remember that he may be able to obtain help from a local Museum's Schools' Service.[5] Not only may he obtain loan exhibits to boost his school collection, but he can draw upon the expertise of museum staff for help with problems of identification and dating.

Worksheets

Teachers may wish to devise worksheets on the objects in their classroom museum. For example, the Second World War thematic display mentioned earlier could be used as a basis for all kinds of work on topics such as rationing or civil defence.

During the project the teacher can devote a lesson to a 'Going for a Song' or 'Animal, vegetable and mineral' programme, in which the children are handed objects or photographs from the collection which they have to identify and discuss.

A Note on Public Collections

For studies of the children's more distant ancestors, the classroom museum is unlikely to be much help and teachers will need to use local and national collections. For Family History, small local museums may be as valuable as the large national ones. Not only do they tend to exhibit the things which are most important for a Family History project (the sort of cooking utensils used by Great-grandmother, for example) but they often have a family intimacy which the sheer size of national museums makes impossible. Some local museums organise courses on topics very closely allied to Family History. For example, the Norwich Museums' Education Officer prepares a programme of lessons for each school session on topics related to local life crafts and industries. These lessons 'are based on actual museum material which in many cases the children can handle for themselves or study closely in the teaching rooms'. The syllabus includes lessons on *Victorian Children: their clothes, amusements, schooling* and on *Victorian and Edwardian Social Background*, excellent material for pupils studying the fourth and fifth generations of their families.

London children are particularly fortunate in that they can call upon the combined resources of the *Victoria and Albert*, the *Geffrye Museum*, the *Science Museum,* the *Imperial War Museum*, the *Bethnal Green Museum*, (which is especially good for toys and dolls), and the *Transport Museum*. However, there are also many specialist collections outside London. They include the *Canal and Waterways Museum* at Stoke Bruerne, Northamptonshire, the *Aircraft Museum* at Biggleswade, the *Montague Motor Museum* at Beaulieu, the *Museum of Rural Life* at Reading; while its superb recreations of domestic interiors and of an Edwardian street make the *Castle Museum* at York of particular interest to the Family Historian.

The current edition of the Index Publication *Museums and Art Galleries of Great Britain* (price 25p) should find a place in the reference section of every history room library. Of course it will not always be possible to visit the museum which will be most useful to the individual child. However, there is no reason why children should not write to the appropriate museums for guide-books, lists of publications and postcards.

Visiting Museums

It is important that children visiting museums should have a clear idea of what they are looking for, so worksheets should be carefully prepared beforehand. These should not be confined to factual instructions but include open-ended questions such as, 'Would you have liked to have . . .?' or, 'Think of 10 household tasks for which your mother uses different tools from those used by your great-frandmother'. Continuity should be emphasised as well as change: 'Find five household objects which have changed very little since great-great-grandmother's time'.

The general aims and approach to museum work have been aptly summed up by Molly Harrison:

> A museum appeals primarily to the senses; the child can be helped to develop visual awareness, sensitivity and discrimination − if he can be encouraged to look, rather than to think that his object is to acquire a collection of facts and nothing more. The wholeness of what he has to keep afterwards is vastly important: a booklet, a frieze, a chart or a model − these are living reminders of his visit, a visual experience he can renew and refer to again and again. A list of facts, a string of answers − these are dead.[6]

The Children's Museum of Family Life

Although there are a growing number of museums which special-ise in domestic interiors and the lives of particular communities, there is as yet no national museum which depicts a cross-section of family life over a number of generations. Even if such a museum dealt only with recent generations, i.e., the early Victorian to the present day, it would soon become a Mecca for schools, particularly if the children were actively involved, as they are at the Geffrye Museum, where young visitors are allowed to wear period clothes and to have space for painting, drawing and modelling. A further degree of involvement might be attained if the children could themselves experience family life in different conditions. For example, they might sit through a tape-recorded air-raid in an Anderson Shelter, or, dressed in Victorian clothes they could be given a lesson on deportment in a Victorian nursery.

Beyond this are more exciting possibilities. Why not a museum in which the children put on their own temporary displays? This museum would hold a stock of household objects, furniture, pictures, clothes and documents as well as books, photographs, slides, films and tapes. Unlike most museums it would not accept an all-the-year-round flood of the general public, but would book whole days to school parties. Each school would be sent a list of possible display themes or asked to nominate its own. When a choice had been made, a brochure containing a comprehensive list of materials on that theme would be sent to the school so that the children could plan in advance what materials they would use and spend their visit setting up their display. They would have to make out proper museum cards and prepare a taped commentary describing their completed exhibition. At the end of the day photographs would be taken and copies later sent to the school. During the holidays, the museum would be open to the public for weekly displays put on and staffed by the best of the previous term's daily exhibitors.

Notes and References

1. Fernhill County Primary School, Farnborough, Hants.

2. Maiden Erlegh County Secondary School, Berkshire.

3. It is perhaps worth noting that against each innovation a prolonged and rearguard action was fought by the teaching and legal professions. Both have now admitted defeat by the ball-point, but the steel-nibbed pen still makes a scratchy last stand at the local bank.

4. We are grateful to our colleague Mr. Harry Strongman for these suggestions.

5. A useful *Guide to School Museum Services*, produced for the Group for Educational Services in Museums, Secretary D.V. Proctor, National Maritime Museum, Greenwich, London S.E.10, lists all local Museum Schools' Services. A list is also included in *The Teachers' Handbook for Environmental Studies* (Blandford, Revised edn., 1971), pp.41-44.

6. Molly Harrison, *Museum Adventure* (1950), p.88.

10 ARCHIVE EXPLORATION

> The students' room at the Record Office itself provides a convincing demonstration of the competence of school children, not all of them of high ability, to study original records, to pursue a theme over a period of time and to present their findings in a form acceptable, not only to their schools, but to professional archivists and to mature research students, who on occasions, have not scorned to refer to a piece of work deposited in the Record Office by a secondary school pupil.
>
> Department of Education & Science, *Archives and Education*, Education Pamphlet No. 54 (1968), p.11.

TEACHERS are often sceptical about children's ability to handle archive material. They forget that every school contains pupils who have already done more sophisticated forms of research in their spare time than they will ever do in school. Children with interests as varied and esoteric as the migration habits of British birds, the watermarks of stamps, South American railway systems, or 17th-century weapons have a reserve of enthusiasm and energy upon which teachers seldom draw. If sent to profitable sources and given sympathetic help, even less able children can produce results which would surprise a teacher familiar only with their performance in routine school work. This has been confirmed by the work of school children in the Essex Record Office, where they now account for a quarter of the total attendances. They are required to adopt a 'professional' approach to their researches: they must give proper references to sources and include in their work a bibliography of primary and secondary source material. The Department of Education and Science comments:

> In terms of persistence, organisation and presentation of material, and the mastery of earlier forms of handwriting, the results are remarkable; but perhaps the most noteworthy feature is the relationship developed between scholarly professional archivists and young students who receive the benefits of the patience, encouragement and, from time-to-time, the salutary challenge, that are at once the weapon and the hall-mark of the good teacher.[1]

Yet children are rarely seen in most record offices, and teachers not much more frequently. Robert Douch comments on the disparity between the number of students and the number of practising teachers that visit record offices. Despite the emphasis which many college history courses place upon the use of primary sources, particularly through work on special studies, there is little evidence to suggest that ex-students apply this principle once they have arrived in the schools.[2]

School Records

Problems of expense, time-tabling, distance and accommodation mean that it is not always easy for even the most archive-conscious teacher to arrange for his pupils to undertake research in record offices, but he may still be able to draw upon valuable school records. One headmaster in the authors' experience discouraged a student on teaching practice from attempting a local study, saying that the material was inadequate. He was blissfully unaware that the school log-book in his drawer (see Plate 64) contained a wealth of detail about the area from as far back as the late 1860s. Of course most schools are too recent to possess records which go back very far but they may be able to borrow records from older local schools. To find out which are the early schools in the area is not very difficult, but one must remember that sometimes the school may have moved from its original premises to a new site, taking with it records such as the register shown in Plate 65.

Increasingly, however, school log-books and other records are being deposited in record offices. The teacher may be able to direct individuals or small groups to consult them there, and indeed such searches are unavoidable when children are seeking information on particular individuals. However, for general background material, the teacher can photocopy representative passages from records. Sometimes the local museum's schools' service or teachers' centre may be willing to undertake the photo-copying.

Where school records are held neither by schools nor by record offices they may be kept at the Local Education Office. This applies particularly to plans of old schools still in use.

School Log-Books

Where a family has been long resident in a district, these log-books will frequently yield names on the child's family tree and will give a personal interest to some long forgotten incident. Even if the names of pupils' ancestors or relatives do not appear, the book will give specific information about the school at the periods they were there. Of course, in most classes today many of the children's families will have come from other parts of the country. Even in these cases, Victorian and Edwardian schools shared a characteristic ethos, which in a sense makes any old log-book relevant to any family. Almost every log-book will provide information about attendances, accidents, punishments, illnesses, inspectors' reports, the health and discipline of the school and the competence of the teachers. Observing a 50 year rule to avoid embarrassment to living people, children can transcribe passages, analyse attendance figures, record reasons for absence from school (such as harvest time or the lack of boots), and learn about pupil-teachers, discipline and payment by results. Here for example

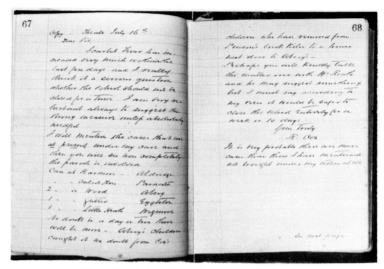

Plate 64. A late Victorian school log book

is an extract from an H.M.I.'s report on Sandhurst School, Berkshire, in 1873:

> There is a mere babel of tongues with lounging and copying in the Infant and Junior classes — ending of course in wretchedly ungrounded results and the work of these lower classes is not well graduated, well methodized or at all skilfully carried out ... My Lords have had great hesitation in allowing any grant at all upon such a report. In so small a school the Mistress has no excuse for neglecting any one child.

This report is followed by the entry on 29 August, 1873:

> I have taken all the children under my own direction except the Infants; Miss Sewell has taught the Infants, I taking them once or twice when I could leave the rest for a short time.

But in January 1874 we find, 'New teacher'.[3]

A report such as this provides a useful stimulus for further work because of the number of questions it poses. What is the grant the Inspector talks about? Why was it so important? Why could not the teacher keep control? What sort of lessons would the children be doing? Was there only one teacher in the school? How many classes were there?

In Church schools there would also be visits from diocesan inspectors. Although by 1872 these were concerned only with religion, their comments throw an interesting light on the plight of some schools:

> Diocesan Inspection. Children presented above 7: 36, under 7: 3, Passed in Reading 35, Writing 33, Arithmetic 32, Dictation 27. The religious knowledge of the two higher standards answered

readily and correctly. The lower standards not so good. The School labours under great disadvantage in not possessing a Classroom. The Books provided are not the best for their purpose. The Discipline is good. The drill very good. The musical instruction shows great care, and very satisfactory results. The result of the Examination, taken as a whole is eminently satisfactory. Both Master and Mistress appear to have done their best.(Buscot School, Berkshire, 1872.)

Sometimes the extracts speak for themselves:

Sent Charles Garraway home as he came without shoes and his clothes and person so filthy. I have been unusually tried this week by the ragged, braceless, buttonless state of some of my boys. Their mothers tell me that the men spend their money in drink that should be spent on the children. Sent one dirty family home but to no purpose, their mother being out to work. (Silver Street Infant School, Reading, 1874.)

It was not always the parents who were drunk. In the Silver Street Mixed School log book two years earlier the two following extracts were found:

Thomas Gough absent all this week, was seen intoxicated in the street on Wednesday Evening.

Friday, J. Prior and J. Huggins absent being in Newbury lock up.

We are not told what their crime was, but Master Huggins or some other member of his family was in trouble again in August 1876:

Harris and Huggins locked up from Wednesday to Friday for stealing fruit.

Presumably not every child would want to acknowledge an affinity with the Hugginses.

There are vivid accounts of tussles between teachers and children, parents and teachers, and in the descriptions of tragic poverty and brutality there are pathetic vignettes of immediate appeal to children. The following stark excerpt comes from what was once a tiny school on the borders of Berkshire and Hampshire. It is now greatly extended, but one can still visit the old school room where the incident occurred:

On Friday a sad incident occurred during the dinner hour. A little girl aged 7 (Alice Murrell) was drying her pinafore at the fire when her clothes caught. She was so severely burned that she died during the night, (Hawley School, 1870.)

In the class which dramatised this episode with a student, there were several little girls who became so involved that they started to cry.

Log books will also supplement and emphasise Victorian and Edwardian memories of discipline, the curriculum, celebrations of Empire Day or military victories, epidemics, and school outings.

School Registers

Another very valuable source, whether the children come from families local to the area or not, is the school register. Many of our older schools have registers going back to the 1850s, when a great many National and British schools were built for the Church of England or the Nonconformist denominations by private bene-factions and public subscriptions. At first sight, the information contained in these registers does not perhaps, seem very promising. However, as with the log-books, a closer scrutiny will reveal a mass of indirect evidence about the children's families. For example, in Plate 65:

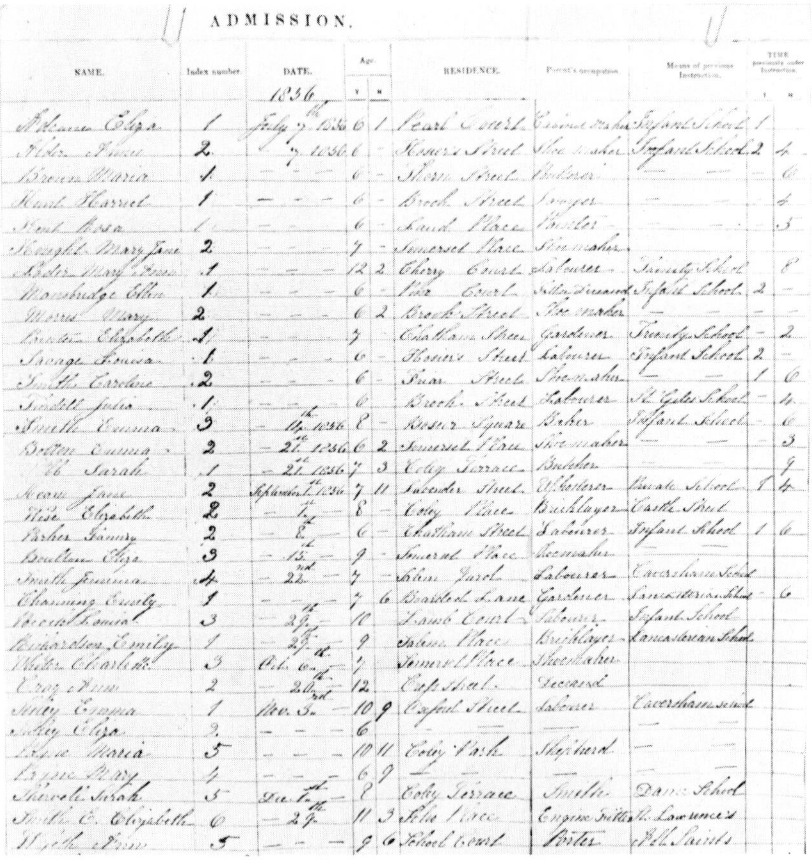

Plate 65. A page from the register of a Church of England School, 1856

1.   Many of the children are quite old by the time they start the school. An extreme example is Mary Ann Loder (number 7). She entered the school aged 12 years 2 months (7 July 1856) and had only been under instruction for 8 months previously.

2.   Among the schools which children mention as having attended previously are a Lancastrian school and a Dame school.

3.   The great majority of fathers are labourers, but there are also two shoemakers, a poulterer, an upholsterer, a baker, a cabinet-maker and a butcher. One is perhaps rather surprised to see in the register of an urban school an entry for the child of a shepherd (6 lines from the bottom). Though now engulfed by Reading, at this time Coley Park was a private estate on the outskirts of the town. Similarly the parent who is an engine fitter (three lines from the bottom) reminds us that we are in the Railway Age.

4.   Out of 34 children, it is interesting to note that in two cases the father is given as deceased.

5.   It looks as if neither residence nor father is recorded in three cases, but closer examination shows that the dashes are to be interpreted as ditto marks both here and in other columns.

Admissions pages should always be used in conjunction with the Withdrawals. For example, in the case of Mary Ann Loder, we find that she left school only three months after her arrival. The reason given is 'Going into Service'. In fact these pages show that few of the children appear to have stopped long at the school. Only a small minority stop longer than a year (7 out of 34). Only one child stops longer than two years — Fanny Parker (16 lines from the bottom). Apart from service, the commonest reasons for leaving school are poverty and the sickness of parents.

Registers of most major (and many minor) public schools have been published. Libraries usually hold copies when the school is in their locality.

Home and School Documents

There is an area of documentation where school and home coincide or supplement each other. Into this category fall school photographs, reports, attendance medals, exercise books, textbooks and school prizes.

Attendance Medals

These appear to have survived in much greater quantities than have early school reports. Again they provide evidence for places, dates and parental attitudes to education.

Prizes, Textbooks, Old Exercise Books

Many homes have treasured old school prizes. These are well worth examining for some have been handed down over several generations. On the whole, textbooks are less interesting, particularly the more common ones. A surprising number of 19th-century readers and story books come to light. Exercise books are rarer

124   *Family History in Schools*

because of their more ephemeral nature, but are more interesting, being more personal.

School Reports

School reports provide evidence not only of academic prowess, or the lack of it, but also of the curriculum followed. Sometimes they are also the only available source of information as to what school an ancestor attended, the dates he was there and what it then was like.

Labour Certificates

Until the Education Act of 1918, pupils who had attained a satisfactory standard at school were allowed to leave at the age of 13. Thus, in marked contrast

Plate 66. School Report, 1927

of today the more intelligent you were the earlier you left. Many of these school leaving certificates or *Labour Certificates* as they were called, survive in private homes.

Plate 67. A Labour Certificate, 1918

School Photographs

For the historian, school photographs not only chart a stage in the individual biography, but provide evidence for the social milieu of the family.

Plate 68. Rural School Photograph (Sulham, Berks. c.1865)

Plate 69. Urban School Photograph (Lambeth, London 1899)

Maps

Modern Ordnance Survey Maps

All pupils should be encouraged to locate their families' successive homes on modern maps. The local library will probably have the Ordnance Survey 1 in. to the mile for the whole country, and a major library may well have the 2½ in. to the mile.

Old 6 in. to the Mile Maps

Period maps should be used wherever possible to make the family's past environment intelligible. The most convenient and manageable series is the 6 in. to the mile, the local edition of which is available at most county and borough record offices and at most reference libraries. If photocopies can be obtained, the pupils can mark on them their relatives' and ancestors' houses, the schools and churches they attended and, perhaps the parks or fields where they played. Some children may wish to mount their photocopy on a board and surround it with photographs taken from the family collection, using different coloured tapes or ribbons to show locations.

Plate 70. Children of St. Cuthbert's school examine the 1845 and 1909 O.S. maps of Pemberton, Wigan, for the places where their ancestors lived and worked.

The first 25 in. to the mile survey (from which the 6 in. to the mile maps were produced by reduction) was 1853-93, although Lancashire and Yorkshire had had a 6 in. to the mile survey between 1840 and 1854. A second edition, or *First Revision*, was produced between 1891 and 1907, a third between 1906 and 1922. This covered most of the country.

1st Edition 1 in. to the Mile

For periods before 1853 (except for Lancashire and Yorkshire) the 1 in. to the mile is the only series available. The 'Old Series' or 1st Edition, consists of 110 sheets, published between 1805 and 1873. Publication began in South-East England, and the Ordnance Survey have republished their 1810 map of the Southampton area. The whole series is currently (1972) being reprinted by David and Charles, Newton Abbot, Devon, price 50p each.

Town Plans

In 1843, the first of the Ordnance Survey town plans — St. Helens — was published on a scale of five ft. to one mile, and during the next half century, three main series of town plans were prepared on scales of five ft. to one mile (1/1056), 10 ft. to one mile (1/528) and 10.56 ft. to one mile (1/500). These show not only individual buildings, but features as small as lamp-posts and horse troughs.

In 1894 the large-scale town plans were discontinued, although in 1911 a new series of 50 in. to one mile town plans was commenced for provincial towns. These have now been replaced by a series produced between 1943 and 1967 which covers all major towns.

Other Maps Normally Found at County Record Offices

Enclosure Maps

These show the redistribution of land as a result of the enclosure of land by private act of Parliament in the late 18th and early 19th century. Although they indicate the land allotted to each landowner, they do not, of course, show the fields into which he may have subsequently divided up his holding. Besides the enclosure map (if it survives), there will be a copy of the act, a schedule showing the new owners and the acreage of their holdings and various associated documents. These often include a map of the parish as it was before enclosure.

Tithe Maps

These were made between 1838 and 1854 after the Tithes Commutation Act of 1836 converted the tithe in kind into an annual fixed payment. In many counties, all parishes were covered. In others, there may be awards for only a third or less of the parishes. Often no tithe award was necessary in the remainder, since enclosure acts had extinguished the tithes at the same time as the land was redistributed. The tithe maps usually show fields with each field numbered. The schedules are the key to the maps, and show the names of each landowner and occupier, the field names, the descriptions of land or premises, the state of cultivation and the acreage, and the rent charged.

Enclosure and tithe maps are usually very big and some record offices cannot photocopy parts of them, but if prior arrangements are made with the archivist, a pupil may be able to trace that part of a map which shows an ancestor's holding. When the tracing is finished an excellent reproduction can be made by putting it in a Xerox machine with a piece of white paper on top of it. The resulting photocopy can be shaded to indicate different landowners.

Estate Maps

Estate maps are sometimes found dating from the second half of the 16th century. However, they are not common for another century, and in some counties not until well on in the 18th century. There may be a whole series for some estates. They are usually on a large scale, and show field boundaries.

Other Maps

Very useful 19th-century town plans will often be found in town histories and guides.

A Three-stage Introduction to Archives

In a Family History project, the pupil is introduced to archives through discovering and using those held by his own family. He becomes the family archivist, busily collecting, sifting, evaluating and commenting upon those records that throw light on his ancestors activities. Next, he explores local records, first those held by his own or a neighbouring school and, later, maps and other topographical sources held by local libraries and record offices. Such documents, which are relevant to both Family and Local history, enable the teacher to broaden his project to include a local study, starting from the memories of the local old people he has previously invited into his classroom. The enthusiast may wish to proceed to a third, more advanced stage, where he studies more specialised archive sources, some of which are described in the next chapter.

Notes and References

1.   D.E.S., *Archives and Education*, Education Pamphlet No. 54, (1968), p.11. For a description of the archive work of one Essex school, *see* F.P. McGivern, 'An Approach to Archives and Local History', *Teaching History*, vol. 2, no. 5 (May 1971), pp.31-2.

2.   Robert Douch, 'Local History' in M. Ballard (ed.), *New Movements in the Study and Teaching of History* (1970), p.108.

3.   This and most of the subsequent extracts from school log books have been taken from Maureen Olive, 'Some Aspects of Elementary Education in Berkshire 1860-1880', a special study (1969) held by Berkshire College of Education History Department.

11 ROOT AND BRANCH

Genealogy may be a bit cranky. Family history is sheer mania.

Nancie Burns, *Family Tree: An Adventure*
in Genealogy (1962), p.15.

A FAMILY HISTORY PROJECT can operate perfectly well using the few generations of the childrens' family about which they have oral evidence or documents available. However, many children express a desire to undertake a more thorough study of the roots and branches of their family trees.

Although the research procedures are within the grasp of secondary pupils, there are two factors which may deter most of them from undertaking more specifically 'genealogical' re-searches. These are expense and inaccessibility. The sympathetic interest of his parents is a *sine qua non* for the schoolboy genealogist. Some parents quickly become even more enthusiastic than their children and they can be invited to the school to talk about the research they have done. It is particularly helpful if such parents can attend any meeting called to explain the aims of a Family History scheme (see above, p. 28).

If only the teacher is in a position to undertake research into more remote ancestors he can share his family with his class. Two Hampshire teachers undertook a Family History project with lower juniors. At the same time they were researching into their own ancestors, had steadily growing family trees on the wall, and dis-played copies of documents they discovered. The children avidly followed the progress of their researches.[1]

Some Useful Guides

The complete beginner with little experience of any kind of historical research has many excellent manuals to show him the way, though not all of them stress Family History, rather than 'mere genealogy'. Excellent from this point of view is Nancie Burns's chatty *Family Tree: An Adventure in Genealogy* (Faber, 1962) in which she tells how she traced her own ancestors and placed them in their historical context. The novice will find more bread and butter information in A.J. Willis's *Genealogy for Beginners* (3rd edn., Phillimore, 1970) which also includes a section on the author's own ancestor-hunt, and Gerald Hamilton-Edwards's *In Search of Ancestry* (3rd edn., Phillimore, 1973) which is particularly strong on the Army and Navy, the other professions, Scotland and India. Less detailed, but wonderful value at the price (30p) is David Iredale's *Your Family Tree* (Shire Publications).

Solutions to particular problems will often be suggested in
D.E. Gardner and F. Smith's very detailed *Genealogical Research
in England and Wales* (Bookcraft, Salt Lake City, 3 vols. 1957,
1959, 1964).

Civil Registration of Births, Marriages and Deaths

The initial stage, which involves obtaining birth and marriage
certificates from Somerset House is particularly expensive — 40p
per certificate, quite apart from any fares involved. For those
living far from London, the information can be obtained by
correspondence, and parents will have to pay not only for the
certificates, but for the research time of the Somerset House
officials. Not may parents will be quite as enthusiastic   as
that. However, these problems can sometimes be overcome
and many teachers and parents have, in fact, taken their children
to Somerset House.

Plate 71. Boys from Stoneham School consult the Somerset House Indexes

The Civil Registration of Births, Marriages and Deaths began on
1 July 1837. This means, however, that one can trace much earlier
ancestors, for if they were married in their 20s in 1837, their fathers,
whose names appear on marriage certificates, were probably born
in the 1780s or 1790s. So, unless a family has only recently
arrived in England or Wales (Scotland and Ireland have their own
registration systems), almost anyone prepared to spend a limited
amount of time and money can track his ancestors into the 18th
century.

How to Begin

a) Oral Information

Maximum information should first be obtained from living relatives. Only too.often people pay for certificates containing information they could easily have obtained from a distant relative. As we have seen, relatives' answers rarely include precise dates, but they can usually offer an approximate one. It is particularly important to discover, if possible, the date when the earliest known ancestor died and how old he then was. A child might, for example, start with a great-great-grandfather who died about 1930 aged about 76.

b) Explaining the Procedures

The way in which births, marriages and deaths are recorded and indexed at Somerset House must be explained in the classroom before a visit.

The Indexes are kept in two separate offices, one dealing with births and the other with marriages and deaths. If an approximate date of death is known, but not the age of the deceased, it is best to start by looking in the index to the deaths. The separate alphabetical indexes to births, marriages and deaths are all arranged by three-monthly periods, and there are often several volumes for each quarter. Searches of the indexes can be made without charge after filling in a form giving such details as one knows. A short search of the death indexes may locate the death of great-great-grandfather in 1928 (not 1930), when he was 80 (not 76). He was thus born in 1848. A search of the birth indexes for 1848 usually will reveal the correct entry rapidly, unless the Christian name and surname were both very common (e.g. John Smith) and the place of birth unknown. Of course, if the ancestor's date of death and age are known with certainty, a search can be made of the birth indexes right away. The index will give the appropriate registration districts and reference numbers for the volume and entry number.

Unfortunately, in England, unlike Scotland, it is not possible to consult the original registration books, and one has perforce to apply for a certificate. This alas, will cost 40p, and involves a wait for the certificate to arrive by post before any further research can be done. For those living far from London, the searching can be undertaken by the staff of Somerset House but this is beyond the means of all but a tiny minority of children.

Reproduced overleaf is an example of an 1848 birth certificate obtained from Somerset House. Boaz Goodman was a London cab-driver and grandfather of one of the authors. In recent years, Somerset House has made xerox copies of the original entry rather than typing it out. Note that the Indexes show not the exact birth-place, but the much larger registration district. Thus though Boaz was born at *Kensworth,* the Index gives *Luton.*

REGISTRATION DISTRICT   LUTON

1845.   Marriage solemnized at in the Primitive Methodist Chapel

in the District of ___ Luton ___ in the ___ Counties of Bedford & Hertford

No.	(1) When married.	(2) Name and surname.	(3) Age.	(4) Condition.	(5) Rank or profession	(6) Residence at the time of marriage	(7) Father's name and surname.	(8) Rank or profession of father.
90	Eighth day of September 1845	David Goodman	Full Age	Bachelor	Straw Plait Dealer	Lower Holloway Parish of Islington,London	William Goodman	Plait Dealer
		Martha Kitchiner	Full Age	Spinster		Burr Street Luton	William Kitchiner	Farmer .

Married in the Primitive Methodist ___ Chapel ___ according to the Rites and Ceremonies of the ___ Primitive Methodists by me

This marriage was solemnized between us, { David Goodman / Martha Kitchiner

in the { William Kitchiner / Mary Ann Kitchiner } presence of us,

Thomas Hobson
W.A.Southam
Registrar

REGISTRATION DISTRICT ___ LUTON

BIRTH in the Sub-District of ___ Dunstable ___ in the Count ies of ___ Bedford and Hertford

1848.

No.	(1) When and where born.	(2) Name, if any.	(3) Sex.	(4) Name and surname of father.	(5) Name and maiden surname of mother.	(6) Rank or profession of father.	(7) Signature, description and residence of informant.	(8) When registered	(9) Signature of Registrar.	Baptismal name if added after registration of birth.
169	Sixth October 1848 9 a.m. Kensworth	Boaz	Boy	David Goodman	Martha Goodman formerly Kitchiner	Carpenter	David Goodman Father Kensworth	Sixteenth November 1848	George Derbyshire Registrar	

Plates 72 and 73. Copies of certificates obtained from Somerset House

Second Visit
Equipped with the information on the birth certificate, the next stage is to search back from 1848 for the marriage of the two parents. This is done by searching in the marriage indexes for the less common of the two surnames, (in this case *Kitchiner*), finding a Martha, noting down the registration district and reference numbers, and then looking to see if there is an identical entry for the other party. This is because it is quite possible that two other Martha Kitchiners were married at different times and in different places, and unless a check is made with the other party to the marriage, you may find yourself applying for a certificate which proves useless.

David and Martha turned out to be married at the Primitive Methodist Chapel, Luton in 1845. Like many early certificates, theirs does not give their exact ages. Many clergy felt that it was impertinent to ask the blushing bride her age.

Further Clues
In most cases, it is not possible to discover from Somerset House the maiden name of the mother of an ancestor born before 1837. It must be remembered, however, that often an ancestor born long before 1837 had a brother or sister born after that date. In Martha's case, family tradition said Boaz Goodman had a maternal uncle Tom, who was younger than he was. After a fruitless search of the birth indexes to 1848 and subsequent years, the quest was extended backwards and his birth entry was found in 1842. (He was in fact six years older than his nephew). Thus from his birth certificate Martha's mother's maiden name was discovered, even though she had been born in 1822, 15 years before civil registration began.

Local Registrars
If the place of birth of great-great-grandfather is unknown, there is no alternative but to obtain the information from the master-indexes at Somerset House. However, if the ancestral locale of the family is known, it is possible to obtain the same certificates at an identical charge from the local registrar. There is no separate index to consult, but as the births, marriages and deaths for each year are indexed at the back of the book, the registrar can usually find relevant entries very quickly. Of course, one may have to go to several registrars in the same area, and it may not be easy to make an appointment with the registrar at a convenient time.

Nevertheless, despite these problems, many may prefer to search locally rather than make a journey to London or pay the fees of Somerset House officials. The registers of Church of England marriages are not held by local registrars, but by the clergy. In some cases these have been deposited with older registers and other parish records in County record offices. The official registers

of Civil, Nonconformist and Roman Catholic marriages are, however, held by local registrars though, of course, denominations may
keep their own unofficial registers as well.

Census Returns

After visiting Somerset House or local registrars' offices, the next
stage is to consult the Census Returns.

The first census was held in 1801, but unfortunately it was not
until 1841 that the enumerator's detailed returns were kept. These
were, until recently, at the Public Record Office, but were moved
to the Land Registry for reasons of space, where those more than
100 years old may be consulted free of charge, provided a search
ticket has previously been obtained from the Public Record Office,
Chancery Lane, London W.C.2.

Increasingly, public, university and College of Education
libraries are obtaining microfilm copies of census returns, so
children whose families are of local origin may be able to consult
the returns of at least one census in a nearby library. However,
an average class will consist of children whose ancestors came from
all parts of the country, and a visit to London will prove unavoidable.

As the 1841 census gave only approximate ages (in five year
groups for persons over 16) and did not include places of birth
(only 'whether or not born in the same county'), it is best to start
with that for 1851, 1861 or 1871. There is a very good chance
that civil registration certificates will supply an address or place
to search for one of these years. In our example, as the information
most urgently needed was the birthplaces of David and Martha, the
first place to look was the 1851 Census for Kensworth, as we know
they were there in 1848. The following entry was discovered.

Name and Surname	Relation to Head of Family	Condition	Age	Rank Profession or Occupation	Where Born
David Goodman	Head	M[arried]	37	Journey-man Carpenter	Beds., Stanbridge
Martha do	Wife	M	28		Beds., Arlsey
Amos do	Son	Un[married]	4		London, St. Pancras
Boaz do	Son	Un	2		Herts., Kensworth
Caleb do	Son	Un	6m		Beds., Cheddington

Since only the middle of the three children was born at Kensworth, the searcher was extremely fortunate to find the Census entry for the family so quickly. Had the family not been located there, it would have been necessary to get a birth certificate of a younger child (the names of the whole family were known from living relatives) born about 1861 and to follow this lead in the following Census of 1861.

The enumerators' returns for Stanbridge were then examined. They revealed:

Name and Surname	Relation to Head of Family	Condition	Age	Rank Profession or Occupation	Where Born
William Goodman	Head	Wid[ower]	63	Straw plait dealer	Beds., Eversholt
Louisa do	Daur*	Un	27	House-keeper	Beds., Stanbridge
Eli do	Son	Un	19	Journey-man Baker	do

* Dau[ghte]r

The 1841 Census filled out the information on this family very considerably. William's wife Mary was then alive, and the children listed were David (25), Carpenter; William (20), Mason: Sarah (20), Dressmaker; Hezekiah (20), Carpenter-Journeyman; Louisa (15); Eli (9), Scholar. The ages of those over 16 were, as has been mentioned, not exact but that of the five-year grouping they were in. Also listed was Sarah Willison (75) with the description 'Parish Relief'. Unfortunately relationships are not given in the 1841 census, but Sarah could well be Mother-in-Law.

The Goodman trail then led to Eversholt, where six households of Goodmans (? Goodmen) were in residence in 1841, and five in 1851, but hardly surprisingly, no venerable Goodman old enough to be William's father. In 1841, one household was, however, headed by Faith Goodman, aged 75 (i.e. 75-80), lace-maker, who later proved to be William's mother. So in the case of the Goodmans, an examination of two censuses took the Goodman Family Tree back to 1788 or, counting Faith, back to 1766!

Besides the genealogical importance of this information, there are many clues here for building up a fuller family history e.g. on occupations, social status, family size and composition. Particularly interesting are the family's moves between country and town.

The searcher was equally fortunate with the Kitchiners. The 1851 census for Arlesey, Beds. revealed, for 58 White Horse Street:

Name and Surname	Relation to Head of Family	Condition	Age	Rank Profession or Occupation	Where Born
William Kitchenor	Head	M	54	Farmer of 22 acres employing 1 man	Herts., Hinxworth
Frances do	Wife	M	50	—	Beds., Henlow
John do	Son	U	24	Baker	Beds., Arlesey
George do	Son	U	18	Farmer	do
William do	Son	U	11	Scholar	do
Thomas do	Son	U	8	Scholar	do
Sarah Green	Niece	U	13	Parish relief	Beds., Clifton
Samuel Green	Nephew	U	9	do	do

This entry was very interesting as it not only gave a most useful lead (to Hinxworth) but:

1.   It provided the name of younger brothers of Martha (who of course did not appear as she was married and living at Kensworth then). William and Thomas were born after 1837, and the birth certificate of either would reveal their mother and hence Martha's mother's maiden name.

2.   It solved a mystery left unsolved by tradition. Apparently Boaz Goodman was friendly with a distant relative called Sam Green. The informant was not clear how they were related or why they should be so friendly. She knew, however, that when his father David Goodman, went off to the Crimean War, Boaz went to live with his grandfather, William Kitchiner. Clearly the evidence of the Census makes it probable Sam Green was still living there as well. Thus although only distantly related to each other, their common kinship with William Kitchiner made them almost adoptive brothers. William seems to have acted as a reception centre for relatives in distress.

3.   Spelling remained fluid until much more recently than is generally realised. Thus William (here *Kitchenor*) died in 1879 and his tombstone describes him as William *Kitchiner*. His son, Thomas who died in 1929 is buried beside him but his tombstone bears the spelling *Kitchener*. Until very recently

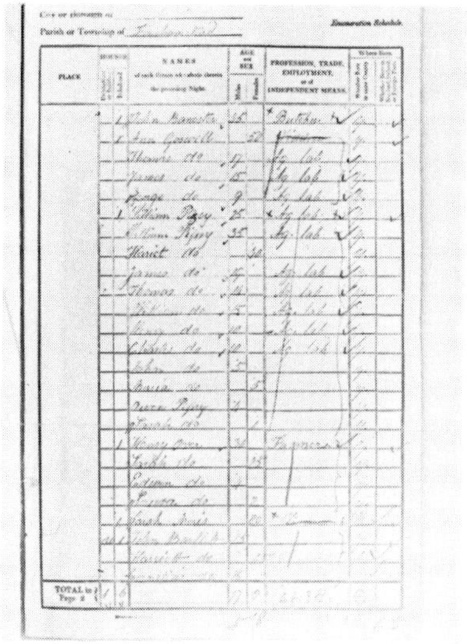

Plate 74. Enumerator's Returns
1841 Census, Finchampstead, Berks.

Plate 75. At work on xeroxes of
the 1851 Census
(Stoneham School, Reading)

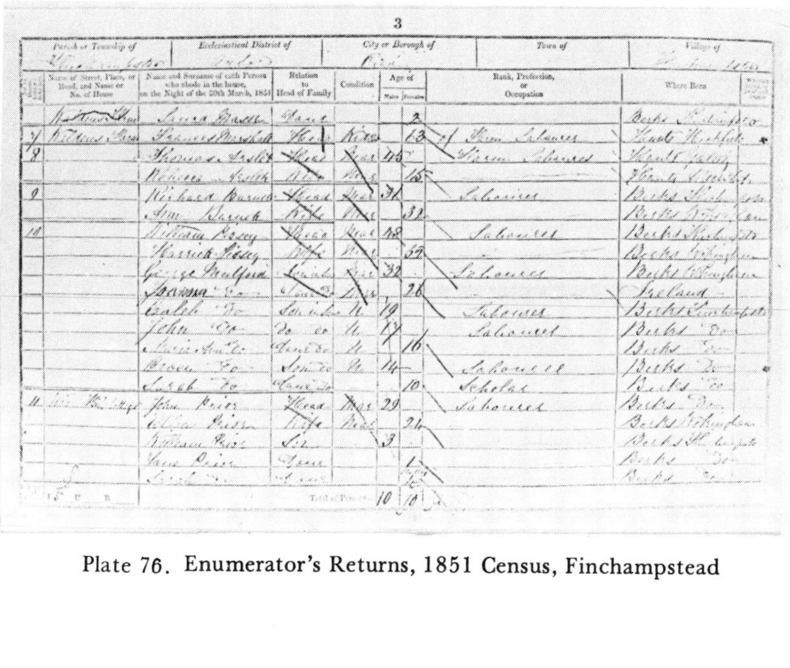

Plate 76. Enumerator's Returns, 1851 Census, Finchampstead

there were grandchildren alive still bearing these two variant spellings. Lord Kitchener's popularity led some branches previously using the 'Kitchiner' spelling to adopt *Kitchener*. However members of other Kitchiner branches are very indignant if their surname is 'mis-spelt' in this way.

It is therefore important that children should not confine their researches merely to persons bearing the same spelling of their surname.[2]

4.   It is interesting to see that as late as 1851, a small farmer was living not in an isolated farmhouse, but in a village street.

The 1841 and 1851 Censuses for Hinxworth revealed four households of Kitchiners, who subsequent research showed were William's brothers or their children. Neither parent of William was apparently still living — at any rate in Hinxworth.

In tracing ancestors from Somerset House and Census Returns, one has to decide whether to trace as many ancestors as possible — a solid block across the board, as it were — or just one line (not necessarily the male line). It is probably best for children to specialize in one line, though pupils should be encouraged to search Census Returns (which can be consulted free of charge) for the households of as many ancestors and relatives as possible, because besides giving them invaluable experience and confidence in using records, this search may introduce them to a good cross-section of Victorian England.

Wills

Copies of all wills proved since 1858 are at Somerset House. Even for relatively recent generations, these can be very useful. Not only may they clarify relationships, but a great deal about a person can be gleaned from his will, such as occupation and social status (e.g. did he own one or more carriages?), business interests, ownership of property elsewhere, personal interests (e.g. he may leave his stamp collection to a philatelist friend or a bequest to the local hunt), religious beliefs (bequests and directions concerning burial), favourite charities, treatment of servants (generous or not), his education (bequests to old school or college), and the pattern of family relationships (most favoured children or relatives). Care should be taken because these are not always accurate indicators. For example, a rich merchant might have handed the family business to his favourite son long before his death and have left him only the 'proverbial shilling'. An unwary pupil might infer a quarrel where all was sweetness and light.

Indexes

There are excellent detailed Indexes to the wills in Somerset House. Very often they give as much information as the wills themselves. This includes the name and address of the deceased, the value of the property left, the names of the executors and the dates the will was made and proved.

These indexes may be consulted free and there is only a modest charge for examining a copy of the will. The original signed will may be produced by special request.

Pre-1858 Wills

Before 1858, the proving of wills was in the hands of the church, and there were a large number of separate jurisdictions. The problems of access, expense and hand-writing put them beyond the reach of all except older pupils whose ancestors lived in the vicinity. An indispensable guide is Anthony J. Camp's *Wills and Their Whereabouts* (Phillimore, 1963).

Parish Registers

After Somerset House and Census Returns the most basic genealogical source is the Registers of Baptisms, Marriages and Burials kept by the parish clergy with varying degree of conscientiousness since 1538. Sometimes still to be found in the parish chest, increasingly they are being deposited in record offices. For further information see the volumes of D.J. Steel's *National Index of Parish Registers* (Phillimore, for the Society of Genealogists).[3]

The Institute of Heraldic and Genealogical Studies, Northgate, Canterbury, Kent, produces a very good series of county maps showing (a) ancient parish boundaries (pre-1837); (b) ecclesiastical jurisdictions for proving wills etc.; (c) starting dates of parish registers of births, marriages and deaths; (d) the position of parish churches (in 2nd edn. only).

Monumental Inscriptions

Although for the most part cut in stone, monumental inscriptions are just as much documents as those written on more usual materials. They are, moreover, the most accessible of the standard genealogical sources. A child who cannot consult Parish Registers deposited in a distant record office, may well be able to persuade his parents to take him to his ancestors' place of origin. Once there, it is quite probable that in the parish churchyard he will find a number of inscriptions recording his ancestors or relatives. If a visit is impossible for the child, those relatives still living in or near the ancestral home-town or village may be unwilling to conduct a protracted search of a register, but quite amenable to looking around the churchyard, copying relevant inscriptions. Even for recent generations, monumental inscriptions may authenticate and supplement information obtained orally.

In general, until the 19th century, clergy and local gentry or dignatories were buried in the church and the common people in

the churchyard. That even in death people stayed in their proper
station is cynically acknowledged in an epitaph at Kingsbridge,
Devon (1795):

> Here I lie at the chapel door;
> Here lie I because I'm poor,
> The farther in the more you'll pay,
> Here lie I as warm as they.[4]

Each part of the country developed its own form of monument.
Bale-tombs distinguish the Cotswolds, table-tombs the West Riding
and brick box-tombs, Kent. Grave-boards, consisting of an inscribed
plank between two uprights are particularly common in Surrey,
Kent and Sussex.

The tombstone often mentions the deceased's place of residence
and sometimes also his trade. It is not uncommon to find several
generations commemorated by one stone.

One great advantage of finding the deaths of all members of one
family recorded together is that the stone may refer to members
of the family who died elsewhere, and who may even have been
buried elsewhere.[5]

Footstones should be studied too. Not only are they sometimes
inscribed with epitaphs, but the initials given on them can often
be helpful in deciphering the headstones.

The Archive Code: Parish Registers and Monumental Inscriptions

Just as children can play a major part in preserving private
documents of all kinds, so can they play a modest part in preserving
more sophisticated archives. Despite the widespread practice of
depositing parish registers in record offices, many still remain in
parish chests, a prey to fire, damp, theft and vermin. Transcription
of these irreplaceable documents is an urgent necessity. The Society
of Genealogists, 37 Harrington Gardens, London S.W.7, will be
pleased to supply both paper and helpful directions and, where
necessary, to smooth the path with a sceptical incumbent.
Because children write slowly, perhaps the most viable method of
transcription for them is to dictate the details into a tape-recorder
and then make a written copy and, later, carefully check it against
the original.[6]

Tombstones, with their memorial inscriptions are as much a part
of history as the parish church and the parish registers. With every
year that passes many more of them are lost and the need to
preserve and transcribe the remainder becomes more urgent.
For many years, the Institute of Heraldic and Genealogical
Studies, Northgate, Canterbury, Kent, has been running a scheme
whereby schoolchildren copy the tombstones in their own
locality. Their leaflet suggests the copying of full details of name,
dates, relationships, occupations, places and other particulars
of all stones commemorating persons born before 1875, and

Plate 77. Tape-recording a Parish Register
(Arborfield Co. Primary School, Berks.)

Plate 78. Copying tombstones
(Arborfield Co. Primary School, Berks.)

emphasises that the sender must ensure that he includes full particulars of the location of the graveyard (parish, postal address etc.). Without this the information, however well presented, will be useless. The Institute offers prizes each year for the best contributions from children: £5, £3, £1, and five runners up. Contributions are judged on completeness of information copied and collected, on neatness and on age. The name, address and age of the transcriber should accompany each copy sent.

In copying tombstones, children can experience something of the excitement of an archaeological dig. Anyone who has experienced the satisfaction of putting together the inscriptions from broken headstones, completely buried and apparently lost for ever, must be surprised that so little work is done in transcribing tombstones and that so much yet remains to be done in this field. Unfortunately the increasing hazards of wholesale destruction leave us so little time in which to do it.

Notes and References

1. Miss Ann Ross and Miss Angela Lythgoe, Fern Hill County Primary School, Farnborough, Hants.

2. On variant spellings see D.J. Steel, *National Index of Parish Registers*, vol. 1 (1968), pp. 138-141.

3. The following volumes have been published to date: Vol. 1. *General Sources for Births, Marriages and Deaths before 1837* (1968); Vol. 2. *Sources for Nonconformist Genealogy and Family History* (1972); Vol. 3. *Sources for Roman Catholic Genealogy and Family History*; Vol. 5. *South Midlands and Welsh Border*. The only county volume published to date, it includes the dates and whereabouts of originals and copies of Parish, Nonconformist and Roman Catholic registers for Glos., Heref., Oxon., Salop., Warws. and Worcs. Vol. 12. *Sources for Scottish Genealogy and Family History*.

4. F. Burgess, *English Churchyard Memorials* (1963), p.20. This is the standard work on tombstones from the artistic point of view. For a thorough examination of the subject from a Family History point of view see D.J. Steel, *N.I.P.R.*, vol. 1. pp.245-270.

5. D.E. Gardner and F. Smith, *Genealogical Research in England and Wales*, vol. 1 (1957), p.44.

6. For an account of work with Primary children see D.J. Steel and L. Taylor, 'Tape Recording of Parish Registers', *Genealogists' Magazine*, vol. 16, no. 9 (1971).

12   THE BOAST OF POWER

> Many barons of proud names and titles have perished like the
> sloth, upon their family tree, after eating up all the leaves; while
> others have been overtaken by adversities which they have been
> unable to retrieve, and sunk at last into poverty and obscurity.
> Such are the mutabilities of rank and fortune.
>
> Samuel Smiles, *Self-Help* (1866 edn.), p.204.

ALTHOUGH MOST CLASSES contain a few children who
find it very difficult to elicit any significant information about
their family's history, there are equally likely to be some
with an ancestor who achieved local fame, and in a surprising
number of cases, was a well-known national figure. For example,
one Primary School class[1] contained a member of the Frere
family which produced Sir Bartle Frere, friend of Edward, Prince of
Wales and Governor of Cape Colony at the time of the Zulu War,
and John Hookham Frere, Minister to Madrid during the Peninsular
War. The child's great-great-grandfather, George Frere, was a Judge
on several commissions for suppressing the slave trade. A rather
different kind of 'famous' ancestor in the same class was, it was
claimed, the McNamara who, with his band, has been immortalised
in song. The great-grandfather of a third was William Hull, the
architect who designed the Corn Exchange and H.M. Prison at
Northampton, the Victoria Station in Manchester and a number
of other public buildings in the North. Three famous ancestors in
one class was rather above the norm, but two seems about
the average.

In another school,[2] a remarkable pedigree was brought in by a
third-form boy. It traced an ancestor's descent from a John West
living in the 17th century. In an accompanying letter the father
sought a place for his son in the Reading Bluecoat School.
A little research soon revealed that John West was the founder
of the school. Thus the father was establishing a claim as founder's
kin. Clearly there was a great scope here for a study of John West
and the school he endowed.

Royal Descents

In the same class another boy produced a royal descent through
the Pastons (see overleaf). This was one of no less than six royal
descents which have been drawn to the authors'. attention
since 1968. Five of these pedigrees were inherited from relatives;
the sixth was discovered through personal research. Of course, such
inherited pedigrees need thorough authentication. However, it is

A ROYAL DESCENT

EDWARD I	= MARGARET of France
Thomas Brotherton Created Earl of Norfolk 1312/13	= Alice dau. of Sir Roger de Hales, Coroner of Nolford 1303-13
Margaret Plantagenet, Countess of Norfolk. Created Duchess of Norfolk, Died 1399	= John, 6th Lord Segrave. Died 1353
Elizabeth Segrave Duchess of Norfolk	= John de Mowbray, 10th Baron Mowbray
Thomas Mowbray 12th Baron Mowbray, Created Duke of Norfolk, 1397. Died 1399	= Elizabeth Fitzalan, dau. of Richard Fitzalan, Earl of Arundel and widow of Sir William de Montagu.
Lady Margaret Mowbray	= Sir Robert Howard of Stoke Nayland, Suffolk
John Howard, Lord Howard. Created Duke of Norfolk and Earl Marshal of England, 1483	= Catherine dau. of Sir William de Moleynus
Lady Margaret Howard	= Sir John Wyndham of Crownthorpe and Felbrigg. Fought at Stoke against Earl of Lincoln & Lambert Simnel, 1487. Condemned for High Treason and beheaded 1503.
Sir Thomas Wyndham of Felbrigg, distinguished naval commander	= Eleanor dau. of Sir Richard Scrope of Upsal, Yorkshire
Mary Wyndham	= Sir Erasmus Paston (ancester of Earls of Yarmouth) son of Sir William Paston (1479-1554), a lawyer and courtier (appears in the Paston papers)
Sir William Paston (1528-1610). Mar. 1551. Founder of North Walsham Grammar School	= Frances dau. of Sir Robert Clere of Stokes by Norfolk
Anne Paston	= Sir George Chaworth of Wiverton
Elizabeth Chaworth. Mar. 1602; d.1635	= Sir William Cope of Hanwell. 2nd Bart. M.P. at various times for Oxford (City), Oxfordshire and Banbury
Jonathan Cope of Rawton Abbey Staffs.	= Anna dau. of Sir Hatton Fermor d.1670
Elizabeth Cope	= John Gouldsmyth (barrister)

Jane Gouldsmyth. Mar. 1718	= George Dod of Highfields, Audlem, Cheshire
Jane Dod of Highfields	= William Baker
Richard Dod Baker of Highfields	= ? Hannah (Hasall?)
William Baker of Highfields	= Ann Hough
George Baker (lawyer)	= Jane Allman
Mary Baker	= Arthur Scutt (farmer)
Mary Scutt	= Kenneth Baines, son of Rector of Slough, known as 'The Sporting Parson, who played cricket for Berks., Bucks., and Oxon, for many years and was President of the three counties Football Assoc. Kenneth himself also played cricket for Berks.
Ruth Baines	= Ian Mantle, Technical Manager, U.K. Fisons, Agrichemicals

Anthony Dod Mantle. b.1955
3rd Form pupil Stoneham School,
Reading, 1968-69.

likely that all are genuine, for it is statistically probable that most of us are descended from the medieval English Kings. For example, the five daughters of Edward I were married to great barons, many of whose daughters and grand-daughters married lesser barons or gentry. Similarly, within a few generations the younger sons of younger sons had become little more than country squires, and their descendants were soon lost in the population at large. Let us take one example. Edward I's daughter, Elizabeth (1281-1316) married Humphrey de Bohun, 4th Earl of Hereford and Essex (died 1321/2); their daughter, Margaret, married in 1325 Hugh de Courtenay, 2nd Earl of Devon (1303-1377) and had eight sons and nine daughters, most of whose descendants were, within a few generations, completely obscure.

Burke in his *Vicissitudes of Families* gives numerous examples of royal descents: the butcher and the toll-gatherer with a proven descent from Edward I, and the cobbler of Newport, Shropshire, who was the great-grandson of Margaret Plantagenet, niece of Edward IV. When Burke was writing, among the descendants of the Duke of Gloucester, son of Edward III, was the late sexton of St. George's, Hanover Square, London.[3]

L.G. Pine quotes the story that J.H. Round, the great genealogist and debunker of spurious Norman descents, one day asserted in conversation that everyone was descended from the Plantagenets. He was promptly challenged to find a royal descent for a labourer working in a nearby field. It is said that he accepted the challenge and proved his point.[4]

The Statistical Probability of a Royal Descent

If we estimate that each of the descendants of Edward I had, on an average, only two children who left issue, over the period of 24 or so generations between Edward's time and ours, this produces a theoretical total of 2^{24} or 16,777,216 descendants living today. If we assume an average of three children each (the correct number is probably somewhere between two and three), the total is the astronomical 282,429,536,481.

Some older, mathematically-minded children may find the statistical aspects of genealogy extremely interesting and be only too delighted to work out problems based on them. At first, they are puzzled as to how there can be more descendants of Edward I than there are English people in the world today. The answer is, of course, that the same descendants appear over and over again through intermarriage. If first cousins married in Generation 2, they would substantially reduce the eventual total. If fifth cousins married they would still reduce it considerably and since most people until quite recently lived in fairly enclosed communities (though less so than was once thought) it was almost impossible for them not to marry close relatives. For example, in the Ayrshire farming family of one of the authors, his grandparents were second cousins and his great-grandparents first cousins. His aunt married a first cousin, so her children, the author's first cousins, instead of having the theoretical 32 great-great-great-grandparents have, in fact, only 16.

If, by any freak of statistical fortune, a child's father had escaped being of royal descent, it is most unlikely that he would marry someone similarly deprived. It must, surely, give children a greater interest in the Anglo-Saxon, Norman and early Plantagenet kings if they realise that in all probability they were their own direct ancestors. As one enthusiastic student of royal descents graphically commented:

> It gives a keener interest to the visitor to Westminster Abbey or Winchester Cathedral, or to the student of English History, if he knows that he is descended in a clear unbroken line from the .kings and great men who lie buried in those sacred fanes and of whom he reads in history, and if he feels that he is united by the ties of blood to the Sovereign of these realms.[5]

It is interesting (and a sad blow to racists) that the World's highest incidence of proven royal descents must be among the

Pitcairn Islanders, the mixed race descended from the Bounty mutineers and their Tahitian womenfolk. Because of inbreeding, all the islanders are now descended from Fletcher Christian, the leader of the mutiny, for whom a royal descent has been established.

Exotic Ancestors

Edward III has been described as the 'Earls Court or Clapham Junction of Genealogy'.[6] Get back to him and you can go where you please: back to Alfred the Great and Ethelred the Unready, to Charlemagne if you fancy an Emperor, or to Rolf the Ganger if you have a taste for Vikings. Every royal descent does, of course, imply that one is descended not only from kings but from all kinds of famous men and women — great magnates, soldiers, statesmen and diplomats. Usually, relationships with famous men such as Drake or Nelson can be worked out almost to order!

The standard work tabulating known royal descents is the Marquis de Ruvigny's five huge volumes entitled *The Blood Royal of Britain*. For exotic branch lines to change on to at Clapham Junction one can consult Turton's *Plantagenet Ancestry*, (reprinted 1969).

Where have all the Barons gone?

Although royal descents can be traced only in the female line, this does not necessarily apply to descents from the nobility, (some of whom in any case were descended from the royal house through many lines). Fuller noted in his *Worthies* that 'some who justly hold the surnames of Bohuns, Mortimers and Plantagenets are hid in the heap of common men',[7] and in the 19th century, if in the countryside the respective stations of the rich man in his castle and the poor man at his gate appeared immutable, in the towns the rapid expansion of a new class of brash, dynamic nouveaux riches gave edge and interest to the decline of old and once powerful families. In *Self Help* Samuel Smiles comments in his chapter on 'Industry and the Peerage' that 'No class is ever long stationary. The mighty fall and the humble are exalted. New families take the place of the old, who disappear among the ranks of the common people'. He notes:

> It is understood that the lineal descendant of Simon de Montfort, England's premier baron, is a saddler in Tooley Street. One of the descendants of the 'proud Percys', a claimant of the title of Duke of Northumberland, was a Dublin trunk-maker; and not many years since one of the claimants for the title of Earl of Perth presented himself in the person of a labourer in a Northumberland coal-pit. Hugh Miller, when working as a stone-mason near Edinburgh, was served by a hod-man, who was one of the numerous claimants for the Earldom of Crauford — all that was wanted to establish his claim being a missing marriage

certificate; and while the work was going on, the cry resounded from the walls many times in the day, of − 'John, Yearl Crauford, bring us another hod of lime'. One of Oliver Cromwell's great-grandsons was a grocer on Snow Hill, and others of his descendants died in great poverty.[8]

It is rather interesting in the light of Smiles's reference to Cromwellian descendants that a teacher undertaking a Family History project should have discovered one of them sitting in his classroom.[9] As Roman Catholics, the family were not particularly proud of the descent, and were much more interested in his mother's descent from the great Irish patriot, Daniel O'Connell.

The same class contained a descendant of the Spencers of Althorp. A diary of the pupil's great-great-great-grandfather, Robert Spencer, reflects the enormous public interest aroused by the Great Reform Act.[10] His kinsman John Charles Spencer, Viscount Althorp, was Chancellor of the Exchequer in Lord Grey's Whig Administration, and his accession to the title of Earl Spencer in 1834 is recorded in the diary.[11]

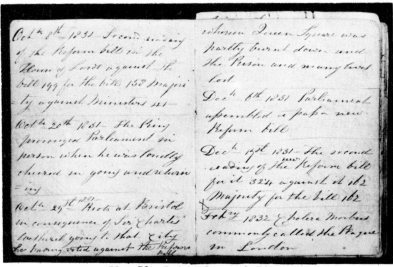

Plate 79.   Robert Spencer's Diary

The disappearance of once powerful families had an equal appeal for that eccentric scholar, antiquary and traveller, George Borrow. While travelling in Wales, he asked directions from a road-man wheeling stones in a barrow. An inveterate philologist, he could not resist asking him his name. 'Dafydd Tibbot', the man replied. As Borrow walked away, he mused on the fall of the mighty:

> 'I'd bet a trifle', said I to myself, as I walked away, 'that this poor creature is the descendant of some desperate Norman Tibault who helped to conquer Powis-land under Roger de Montgomery

or Earl Baldwin. How striking that the proud old Norman names are at present only borne by people in the lowest station. Here's a Tibbot or Tibault barrowing stones on a Welsh road, and I have known a Mortimer munching poor cheese and bread under a hedge on an English one. How can we account for this save by the supposition that the descendants of proud, cruel and violent men — and who so proud, cruel and violent as the old Normans — are doomed by God to come to the dogs?'12

Readers of Hardy will remember how the plot of *Tess of the D'Urbervilles* hinges on the same theme. Clearly, it must have been the following passage from Camden's *Remaines Concerning Britaine* (1605) which suggested both the idea and the name:

> Neither is there any village in Normandy that gave not denomination to some family in England; in which number are all names . . . beginning or ending with . . . *Vil*, which is corruptly turned in some into *Feld*, as in *Baskerfeld, Somefeld, Dangerfeld, Trublefeld, Greenefeld, Sackefeld,* for *Baskervil, Somervil, Dangervil, Turbervil, Greenevil, Sackvil.*13

Although royal and noble descents are much more numerous than most people suppose, the foregoing must not be interpreted as indicating that just because a person has a well-known surname, such as Howard or Russell — or even Mortimer — that he is connected with the aristocracy. Howard, for example, was a not uncommon personal name (it is a variant of Hereward), and the majority of Howards, like most families with less aristocratic-sounding names doubtless descend in the male line from medieval peasants. However, the probability is that the majority of Courtneys or Courtenays are descended from the Earls of Devon, and most Seymours from the Norman family of St. Maur. With families like the Irish Fitzgeralds, we are on shakier ground, as their chiefs, like their Scottish counterparts, acquired followings who took their name. Any descent, whether through the male or female line must be fully authenticated before a claim is accepted.

Famous Ancestors

Of course the proportion of children with an authenticated royal descent (or one relatively easy to establish) must be very small. However, many cases of famous ancestors must be constantly discovered by teachers through chance remarks by children. Many more are completely overlooked unless brought to light through a Family History project. As we have remarked, one boy was descended from Oliver Cromwell though his father, and Daniel O'Connell through his mother. Irish patriots seem popular ancestors. At another school, an eight-year-old asked one of the authors if he had heard of Michael Davitt. Fortunately, he had. The child volunteered the information that she was a direct descendant of the Fenian leader, and that the name Michael Davitt had been inherited by her brother. Her parents had, she said, a biography of her ancestor which she kindly offered to bring to school. Until this chance remark, the class teacher had been quite unaware of the interesting connection. Similarly, working with children from a local school on a quite different type of project, the same author discovered that the grandparents of one of the children formerly owned Bulmershe Court, the mansion on the site of which the authors' college now stands.

It is extraordinary how often one chances upon famous ancestors. The sociologist, Mary Farmer, has noted:

> Among long-established members of the middle class there is often kin knowledge in greater depth. Many seem to claim descent, and indeed are able to produce relics, passed down in the family, from personages who had some claim to fame in their own generation such as a minor poet or explorer of the eighteenth or nineteenth century.[14]

This is borne out from the authors' experience. One child proved to be a descendant of Dr. Benjamin Hoadly, Bishop in succession of Bangor, Hereford, Salisbury and Winchester (1676-1761), and singled out by Rupert Davies as the extreme example of episcopal indifference to his duties:

> Some bishops scarcely thought it worthwhile to visit their dioceses at all, though few, if any, were as remiss as Benjamin Hoadly, Bishop of Bangor for six years and of Hereford for two, and never seen in either place — but then, his writings show that he saw no real need for a visible church, for orders, for sacraments, or for discipline.[15]

The child's mother was able to muster an 18th century engraving of a portrait by Hogarth, his signet ring and seal and a commemorative medallion struck a year or so after his death. Her husband, not to be outdone, claimed a traditional, but unproven connection with Thomas Moore, the Irish poet.

It seems likely that most people with an illustrious forebear are aware of it, though the exact line of descent may have been forgotten; thus one leather-jacketed ton-upping teenager knew that he had an ancestor who 'wrote a book'. The ancestor turned to be Bishop Stubbs![16] Similarly, a relation by marriage of one of the authors, a watch repairer named Benbow who died in poverty in Brixton in 1946, claimed to be a descendant of Admiral Benbow, and indeed had documents proving his title to the use of the family vault, though his widow did not take advantage of it. In her own right she received a small quarterly sum from a fund for poor relations set up by a Wiltshire landowning family early in the 19th century. Here is an example of a couple living in poverty, both of whom had wealthy connections.

At one Primary School[17] the two 'famous' ancestors in a fairly typical class were Henry Schultess-Young, a barrister prominent in the campaign against compulsory vaccination, and Spurgeon, the famous Baptist preacher. The descendant of Schultess-Young brought to school an enormous scrapbook of cuttings about his forbear's activities. Spurgeon's descendant, like that of Michael Davitt (see p.149) brought a biography.

Local Worthies

Many children have ancestors or connections who achieved local, if not national, fame. They may have been mayors, aldermen, county councillors, clergy, solicitors, village schoolmasters, trade unionists, army and navy officers or prominent local businessmen. In many cases, children will bring newspaper and other documents about their activities. Where the families are local, these can be amplified by research in the files of local newspapers. Obituary notices often give informative biographical summaries. One great-grandfather, who had risen to the rank of Sergeant-Major in the regular army and had served in India, the Boer War and the First World War, had a massive funeral attended by the officers and men of his old regiment. The article contained three photographs of the funeral. Some children's parents or grandparents may have been associated with well-known exploits in the War, like the father who had taken part in the famous 'Dam-Buster' raid.

Prominent Sportsmen

Many classes will produce a connection with a sportsman who achieved county or even international honours. The grandfather of one boy was one of nine brothers, all of whom became golf professionals, and one of whom was President of the Professional Golfers' Association. The boy attached many newspaper cuttings to his project. Such connections should not be despised. Many children much prefer a sporting ancestor to a mayor or a minor politician.

Criminal Ancestors

If there are so many descendants of famous ancestors scattered through our classrooms, it seems probable that there are almost as many descendants of infamous ones — criminals of one kind or another, bankrupts, deserters, bullies, cheats, gamblers, drunkards and bigamists. Yet out of over 700 children and students who have undertaken Family History projects, not one has boasted of such an ancestor. One cannot but suspect that there has been a wholesale suppression of some of the most intriguing information. However, perhaps Australian teachers might have more success!

Some Useful Reference Books

Any child fortunate enough to have an established pedigree, or who is told about a famous ancestor or relative should be directed to go to his local library and look in the *Dictionary of National Biography.* (22 vols. to 1901. Supplements to 1971). Also very useful are J. Foster's *Alumni Oxonienses* (8 vols. 1887-92) and J. and J.A. Venn's *Alumni Cantabrigienses* (10 vols. 1922-54) which give brief biographies of Oxbridge graduates. Other specialised biographical dictionaries are:

Colvin, H.M., *A Biographical Dictionary of English Architects, 1660-1840* (1954).
Delany, J. and Tobin, J.E., *Dictionary of Catholic Biography* (1962).
Foster, J., *Index Ecclesiasticus [1800-1840]* (1890).
Gillow, J., *A Literary and Biographical History or Bibliographical Dictionary of English Catholics*, 5 vols. (1885-1902).
Grove, Sir G., *Dictionary of Music and Musicians*, 5th edn. 9 vols. (1954).
James, G.F., 'Collected Naval Biography', *Bull, Inst. Hist. Research* vol. 15, p.162 (1937-8).
Judd, G.P., *Members of Parliament 1734-1832* (1955).
Kirk, J., *Biographies of English Catholics in the 18th Century* (ed. J.H. Pollen & E. Burton) (1909).
Ralfe, J., *The Naval Biography of Great Britain*, 4 vols. (1828).
Redgrave, S., *Artists of the English Schools* (1878).
O'Byrne, L.R., *A Naval Biographical Dictionary* [of officers serving in 1845] (1849); *Naval Biographical Dictionary*. Vol. I and part of Vol. II (1861).
Slonimsky, N. (ed.), *Baker's Biographical Dictionary of Musicians* (1958).

If not only isolated individuals but the family as a whole was a well-known one, or held land, the child should be directed to *Burke's Peerage* and *Burke's Landed Gentry*, both of which are on the reference shelves of most public libraries. A large number of family histories have been published. These are listed in T.R. Thomson, *A Catalogue of British Family Histories* (2nd edn. 1935, new ed. scheduled for 1973). Equally useful are the two massive volumes of indexes to printed pedigrees: G.W. Marshall's *The Genealogist's Guide* (1903) and J.B. Whitmore's *A Genealogical Guide* (1953). These are available in major libraries.

Immigrant Families

It must not be assumed that children of immigrant parents lack interesting ancestors. Many of the immigrants belong to races much more family conscious than the English, and there is certainly no need to adopt a defeatist attitude. Many Jewish children have well-authenticated pedigrees from prominent Sephardi families.

Father knew Lloyd George

Although most children cannot claim a famous ancestor, almost all will have had a forebear or relative, who at one time or another had a connection with somebody famous. In many cases, a member of the family will have been his servant or employee, or may

THE MOORE FAMILY

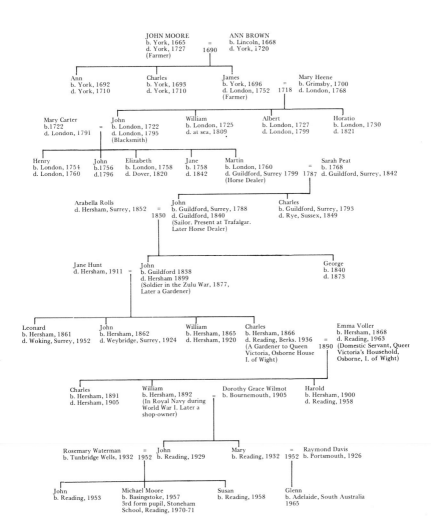

An interesting pedigree from a Family History project in a Reading secondary school. Note the Servicemen at Trafalgar, the Zulu War and the First World War, Queen Victoria's domestic servants, the London blacksmith (a reminder that not all blacksmiths were rural) and the family moves (5 places of residence in 300 years)

have served under him in the Forces. One pupil was the great-grandson of one of Queen Victoria's gardeners at Osborne and his wife, a lady's maid there (see p.153), while a College of Education student wrote her special study on Thomas Hardy's doctor, her great-grandfather. Sometimes the connection with the great is even more tenuous. 'He often visited the shop where my Mum used to serve', a child might say. One should not despise these contacts. Such memories are often very vivid and a source of entertaining anecdotes. As Dr. Fines has pointed out, 'Family History does not forget the great events and personalities of national history . . . In innumerable cases, father really did know Lloyd George and has a worthwhile memory of him'.[18]

Notes and References

1. St. Theresa's R.C. Primary School, Wokingham, Berks.

2. Stoneham School, Reading.

3. Sir J.B. Burke, *Viscissitudes of Families* (1859), quoted in Samuel Smiles, *Self Help* (1866 edn.) p.203.

4. L.G. Pine, 'Royal Blood in the People of Great Britain', in *The Amateur Historian*, vol. 1, no. 6, (1953), p.166.

5. W.G.D. Fletcher, *Royal Descents* (1908), p.5.

6. L.G. Pine, *op. cit.*, p.166.

7. Smiles, *op. cit.*, p.203.

8. *Ibid.*

9. Maiden Erlegh School, Berkshire.

10. For another entry from this diary, see above p. 73.

11. We are grateful to Mrs. E.M. McKinlay (nee Spencer) for the loan of this interesting diary for photocopying and for permission to reproduce the extracts in Plates 16 and 79.

12. George Borrow, *Wild Wales*, World's Classics edn. (1862), p.427.

13. William Camden, *Remaines Concerning Britaine* (1605), pp.95-96.

14. Mary Farmer, *The Family* (1970), p.35.

15. Rupert E. Davies, *Methodism* (1963), p.29. In the book he is called George by mistake.

16. The authors are indebted to G.R. Humphrey-Smith, Director of the Institute of Heraldic and Genealogical Studies, for this story.

17. St. Dominic's R.C. Primary School, Woodley, Berks.

18. Dr. J. Fines, 'Family History — Its Case, Place and Resources', Conference on Family History in Schools at the Berkshire College of Education, 4 September 1970.

13 TEACHERS' REPORTS
1: Family History with Younger Pupils

The outstanding feature of the project was the way in which it totally involved my whole class: tough Mark, timid Elaine, lively Paul and sleepy Stephen! The children attacked their tasks with unprecedented enthusiasm and experienced a novel sense of pride in their work.

> Mrs. N.C. Bevan, Meadowvale County Primary School,
> Bracknell, Berks. (1971).

OUR FAMILY HISTORY SCHEME has proved flexible enough to be used successfully with Junior School classes of 40; a family group of 90 children aged 9 - 11; with a Secondary Modern School unstreamed year-group of 120; with Grammar School classes of 30; with smaller groups of school leavers and with a cross-section of students and adults. We conclude our book with reports from some of those who have taken part in the scheme.

In each case, after preliminary discussion, the teachers were encouraged to develop the scheme as they thought best — there was no attempt to impose any detailed structure upon them. It is interesting that, despite their differing aims and emphases and their differing problems, all the projects developed along roughly similar lines and revealed similar weaknesses of organisation and resources. Most teachers moved from a relatively unstructured project to a fairly highly structured one, though pupils were still allowed the maximum possible choice.

A 'WHO AM I?' PROJECT
with 1st and 2nd year Juniors (Aged 7-8 and 8-9)
Miss Ann Ross and Miss Angela Lythgoe,
Fernhill County Primary School, Farnborough, Hants.

When Ann Ross and Angela Lythgoe first suggested undertaking a *Who Am I?* project with seven-and-eight-year-olds, we had reservations, for no one had previously attempted any part of the Family History scheme with such young children. However, these two teachers developed the *Who Am I?* phase of the scheme considerably, and it is mainly due to them that this project became not just an introduction to the more specifically historical stages of the scheme, but a valuable project in its own right, particularly suited to the needs of younger children. One point that emerges clearly from their work is that, with this age group, the emphasis needs to be on oral, pictorial and graph work rather than on writing.

Report

We had two unstreamed first and second year junior classes working together. Our starting point was the children's knowledge of themselves and what they could learn about themselves from their families or from documents (e.g. birth certificates). The children were encouraged to bring to school personal relics such as toys and photographs. From here they worked both backwards and outwards, looking at both the family unit and the locality. This work took the best part of the Autumn term.

At the end of the term, a child-inspired questionnaire involving the wider family circle was sent out, in the hope that the Christmas family festivities would provide a meeting point for relatives. After the holidays the information was correlated in group and class sessions by means of individual recording, retrographs, a card-index system and displays. Children with difficult home backgrounds had their enthusiasm channelled into the more social aspects of the work, e.g. a study of toys.

The children were encouraged to write letters to relatives, seeking information. The answers to these and the information given by parents provided points of interest for discussion and comparison.

Apparatus
1. Hand-made, loose-leaf files, entitled *Who Am I?*;

2. Questionnaires and Contents pages, duplicated in order to help children to overcome the problem of excessive writing.

3. A joint display area available to both classes at all times, for which most of the items were provided by the children.

Conclusions

The children's enthusiasm proved that the work was successful as far as it went, though many possibilities remained unexploited. However, by the third term, the children were unable to sustain a high degree of concentrated interest and the second years branched out into a local study.

The greatest problem was the children's inability to write quickly enough to keep up with their enthusiasm. Another limitation was the dearth of suitable books on modern social history designed for this age group. However, this problem was largely overcome by the children's setting up their own card-index of the information they had collected. The retrographs (see p. 42) were a great success, and helped the children with their concept of time.

We both felt that this work was worthwhile with this particular age group, as it gave the children a deeper understanding of themselves in relation to their environment. We are sure that it could be resumed at a later date without detriment to the children's enthusiasm and without duplicating areas already explored.

INTERDISCIPLINARY PROJECTS
with 3rd and 4th year Juniors (Aged 9 - 11)

Harry Strongman, Senior Lecturer in History, Berkshire College of Education, in collaboration with:
Mrs. Bentley, Mrs. Paddick and Messrs. Howard and Wilkinson (Micklands County Primary School, Lower Caversham, Oxfordshire) Alan Coleman and Mrs. Phyllis Spence (The Hill Primary School, Reading), assisted by students of the Berkshire College of Education.

The main interest of both of Harry Strongman's teams was to explore the interdisciplinary possibilities of Family History. The experiments are noteworthy both for the number of teachers involved and for their validation of work-sheets.

Extensive work on Family History also has been done with older Primary School children by Brendan Murphy and Mrs. Darwin at St. Cuthbert's R.C. Primary School, Wigan. It is described in Mr. Murphy's article, 'History Through the Family', in *Teaching History*, vol. 2, no. 5 (1971).

Report by Harry Strongman

When I joined the Berkshire College of Education, I found my colleagues were in the process of evaluating a number of Family History projects undertaken in primary and secondary schools. I offered to mount an experiment with a group of Primary School teachers in order to devise ways of overcoming certain specific problems and to explore the interdisciplinary possibilities more fully than had been done hitherto.

The First Experiment, 1969-1970: Four Classes of 9-11 year olds
In the first of the preliminary discussions with the teachers of Micklands County Primary School, it was agreed that we should concentrate on finding solutions to three problems, namely (a) how to bring together in a meaningful way the mass of material each child collected; (b) how to relate this information to the general historical background; (c) how to provide for children who, for one reason or another, found it difficult to obtain enough family material to work on.

Our solution to these problems was to introduce a focal point for the Family Histories. This was a Patch study of the year 1945. The reasons for selecting this particular year were many and varied, but foremost among them was the fact that 1945 was during the lifetime of the children's parents and the pupils would therefore have ample opportunities for collecting oral and written evidence. The Patch study also offered considerable scope for group assignments and discussions and provided a coherent theme

for an end-of-term exhibition. Those children who, because of
unco-operative parents, or special problems, experienced difficulty
in obtaining material, were able to use information collected by
others. Thus, our first objective was satisfactorily achieved.

Our second objective was to discover how a group of teachers,
each with his or her own specialised knowledge, experience and
interests, could exploit and develop the interdisciplinary potential
of Family History. We held weekly staff discussions on different
aspects of the chosen period and considered how the available
material could best be deployed. All the teachers undertook work
in subjects outside their own speciality as well as within it and
eventually almost every school subject was brought into the scheme.
For example, one teacher with a special interest in mathematics, saw
the possibilities of using for statistical and graph work the information the children had collected on prices and incomes in 1945.

Nevertheless, we did not feel we had fully exploited the
interdisciplinary potential of the scheme. There were three reasons
for this: one term did not give us enough time to develop the
project; its scope was too wide, despite its being limited to one
year; there were insufficient resources for the 120 children who
were taking part.

*The Second Experiment, 1970-1971: A Group of 20 10-11 year
olds, working within a team — teaching situation involving 2
teachers and 60 pupils*

This experiment differed in two important respects from the
first: the teachers of The Hill School worked as a team instead of
with independent classes and the project was undertaken by only 20
volunteers, while the other pupils worked on different projects.
Apart from these differences, the experience of the previous year
led me to make important changes both in the form of the
project and in methods of resourcing it.

Structure

The project was planned for a whole year, instead of for a term
and included three Patch studies of the years 1945, 1914 and 1870,
instead of only one. Family memories would be few for 1870, but
we chose that year because a wealth of material was available in
connection with the centenary of the 1870 Education Act. We
probably made a mistake, for the work of this part of the project
tended to move away from the experience of the children's
families. 1901 would therefore probably have been a better year to
have chosen.

While the chronological extent of the project was increased, its
area was reduced by being concentrated upon Reading and
Caversham. Though the aim — to produce an integrated Family

History and Local History project — was a valid one, we were probably mistaken in giving the work such a narrow geographical base. In the first two Patch studies it proved impossible to keep strictly to the local theme — some of the most interesting family experiences took place elsewhere. For example, the father of one boy was the British Military Commandant in Berlin in 1945 and married a German refugee from East Prussia. On the other hand, the 1870 Patch became an almost wholly local study as the only child who could produce many family documents for this period was the one with the German mother. His cache of papers dealt with life in East Prussia under Kaiser Wilhelm I.

We made more use of assignment cards than we had in the previous project, so the children's individual work was much more highly structured.

Resources

The problem of a dearth of resources was overcome by the preparation of a large information bank. Small groups of students who were involved in the project, saved us weeks of work by making sets of information cards and folders.

The 1914 Patch study was resourced by making folders of extracts from Purnell's *History of the First World War* and from various editions of *Knowledge*. These provided plenty of material, but less able pupils found them rather difficult. The folders were supplemented by material, such as old newspapers, made available by Reading Museum Schools' Service, and a number of facsimile posters from the Imperial War Museum. These provided a focus for numerous wall displays which aroused much interest throughout the school.

Interdisciplinary Work

The context of an integrated day allowed work to flow smoothly from one subject to another. For example, one group of children carrying out a study of Air Raid Precautions, discovered an Anderson shelter in a Caversham garden. They measured it and built a large-scale model of it in corrugated cardboard.

This exercise in art and craft posed a series of technical problems. The children's difficulties in bending the corrugated cardboard to the required shape led them to consider how corrugated iron was bent. Once the model was completed, its strength was tested by dropping a number of different sized weights from various heights both on the Anderson shelter and on a building with a flat corrugated cardboard roof. In this way the children were led to consider the resistance of an Anderson shelter to blast and falling masonry. To complement the model, the children obtained a number of accounts of life in an Anderson shelter and wrote and produced a play based on their research. The whole Anderson shelter mini-project was completed within a week. This kind of intensive activity was to be seen again and again in each term of the project as the children's interest was caught by different items of information they collected from parents, grandparents and from people they interviewed in the Caversham area.

In general, the second project was much more successful than the first. Interdisciplinary possibilities were more fully exploited and the inclusion of three Patch studies enabled interesting comparisons to be made between them, although these could have been planned in more detail and discussed more thoroughly. Experience showed that the machinery for this should be built into the basic structure, rather than dealt with on an *ad hoc* basis. Nevertheless, both the structuring and the resourcing were much better than in the previous project. Though the marriage of Family History and Local History was not entirely successful, the proven advantages of a combined scheme were sufficient to justify further experiments in this direction.

AN INTERDISCIPLINARY PROJECT
with an unstreamed 1st year Secondary Modern School Class
(Aged 11-12)
Chris Stafford (Project Controller), Hedley Rogers (Head of the Lower School), Mary Figg (Art), Susan Denton (Drama) Maiden Erlegh School, Berkshire, 1970-1971

The experience of the Maiden Erlegh team is of particular interest because they were undertaking the project with such a large number of unstreamed Secondary Modern school children. Their work was featured in *Family History*, the first of the B.B.C. television series, *History on the Rack*, screened in October 1971.

Report by Chris Stafford

The project was undertaken over two terms with 120 unstreamed first year Secondary Modern children, divided into two working groups of 60, each with a half-day a week with two members of staff — an English teacher and a geographer. In addition, there was specialist help in art and drama. Although no member of the team was a specialist historian, we all felt that a Family History project could provide the cornerstone for integrated work.

A Team-Teaching Situation
When the scheme was first mooted, we made several fundamental decisions:

1. There must be a recognised project-controller to ensure that the work of the team was fully co-ordinated.

2. Specialists must feel confident that their subjects were an integral part of the scheme and not ancillary to a project conceived in terms of another discipline. Similarly the children were not to be encouraged by any member of the team to regard the project as 'history' or even to think in terms of 'subjects'.

3. It was therefore important that subject specialists should be associated with the project at the very beginning of the planning stage, and must play a full and creative part in its development.

The importance of these points became apparent in the enthusiasm of the art and drama specialists throughout. Much of the work was during time allotted to art and drama, and the children carried it over into time allocated to the project. A useful bonus occurred when, during the project time, the drama specialist was able to involve groups of 5th year pupils in working with the first year. This was a two-way traffic — the 5th formers were given responsibility and had raw material on which to develop their ideas, and the younger children gained from working in small groups.

Working Conditions

We were very fortunate in that our working conditions were almost ideal. We had the use of a big self-contained open-plan ROSLA unit, consisting of two large working areas suitable for formal work such as lectures or films; a smaller room suitable for

Plate 80. The working area. Maiden Erlegh School

interviewing, for tape-recording or for groups to use a filmstrip or overhead projector; and many work bays, which were used for art-work, craftwork and for the Classroom Museum.

Plate 81. Family History in Progress,
Maiden Erlegh School

Historical Aspects

Although the project was fully interdisciplinary, we felt that the more specifically historical values were not neglected. Although we did not devise any objective form of assessment, we felt throughout that the children were getting a real feeling of involvement in the past. This could be gauged not only from their enthusiasm, but from the way the atmosphere of a bygone age was caught by much of the work — particularly the stories, poems, letters, painting and drama.

The retrograph (see p.42) was found particularly useful. The children took a great pride in its appearance and they soon became proficient in deducing information from it (e.g. how old parents and grandparents were when the Second World War started, or what was happening when Dad was a similar age to them). It was perhaps a mistake for them to number all years on each bar. Not only was this very time-consuming, but the detail tended to obscure the main purpose of the retrograph — to show people's relative life-spans and generational overlap. On the other hand, children of very limited ability found it much easier to go back one year at a time on each bar than to construct the whole bar at once. In such cases, it may be best to continue numbering all years, if only temporarily, in pencil. Certainly ages should be shown for key dates.

Many children found difficulty in constructing family trees. It became apparent that more detailed instructions are necessary to ensure that only one ancestral family is shown on a tree and that the separate generations stand out clearly.

Classroom Museum

The Classroom Museum was begun in the Spring term. Children were encouraged to bring in items each week, talked about their objects to the rest of the group and completed record cards. Thematic displays were set up from time to time (e.g. coins and medals, schoolbooks and clothing). We were very fortunate in being able to borrow two large museum display cabinets from Reading Museum Schools' Service, who expressed interest in the whole idea. The Classroom Museum was undoubtedly one of the most successful features of the scheme.

Parental Involvement

Half a term was spent on the *Who Am I?* stage of the project. The children became intensely involved, and most parents were helping in various ways at home. In the second half of each Autumn term, the school has a parent interview week in which each parent is allocated an interview time and has the option of attending with the child — a more demanding but more rewarding arrangement than the usual 'Parents' evening'. It has been found by experience that given an interview date and time, even apathetic parents often turn up. This was the ideal context in which to talk to parents individually about the Family History scheme, and they were given a personal invitation to come to a meeting when the project would be explained in more detail. There was about a 65% response to this meeting, and many who were unable to come expressed interest. In the following term, the children took home a continual stream of letters, questionnaires, survey sheets and requests for museum displays, keeping parents aware of what the children were doing.

Involvement of Elderly Relatives and Friends

Every effort was made to encourage children to contact their elderly relatives, either personally or by letter. Those in the vicinity of the school were invited to come in during the project in order to talk to the children.

Several visits were made to Old People's Homes. For the first visit, a parent who was a greengrocer was kind enough to donate fruit for the children to take, which provided an *open sesame*. The children had to be very carefully prepared as some old people were rather suspicious, and others very short with the children. Clearly such visits must be carefully planned, and groups must be small.

We hope to develop this idea much further next year. Ways are being explored of combining a Family History project with social service work of various kinds. It is hoped that children with particular family difficulties can 'adopt' and 'be adopted by', a local old person.

The Patch

It was decided to undertake a Second World War patch as an integral part of the project. This was planned in detail and strongly emphasised the imaginative reconstruction of personal situations.

Problems

The greatest problem to be overcome was the difficulty two people had in trying to gain a good knowledge of the particular points of interest in 120 Family Histories and to supervise 60 of these at one time. In theory, what was required was the intensity of supervision that students have working on theses or special studies. This clearly is impossible in schools with present staffing ratios. As the project went on, it was therefore necessary to impose a much more formal plan than had originally been contemplated. We found that in order to keep 50 children busily working while 10 of the less able were given more intensive help, it was necessary to devise and use very specific task sheets, though the most able were always given freedom to use their own initiative. It also proved essential to give clear short-term objectives, as in the early stages, many of the children became confused by the sheer immensity of the project. The work therefore was broken down into units.

The other major problem was lack of resources. This was mainly overcome by compiling about 150 folders of material. The majority of the children found completing information cards very laborious, so we did not achieve any significant pooling of information, although we had about 15 very detailed accounts of life in the past written by parents, grandparents and other relatives. These were not fully used even by the pupils who had obtained them. Clearly, rather than expecting these children to make numerous information cards, we should have obtained their relatives' permission to photocopy the accounts, cut them up and mount them on cards. Next year, with a capital of worksheets and folders of material already prepared, we shall have more time available for this kind of work.

Conclusion

All members of the team feel that Family History makes a very valid contribution to the theory and practice of Secondary education. It can provide valuable groundwork for a Humanities course and is an excellent vehicle for bringing about closer relations between home and school.

14 TEACHERS' REPORTS
2: Family History with Older Pupils

Why does your own family seem so interesting? I have found this project not as work, but as enjoyment and pleasure. People say it does not matter if we know who our ancestors were or not, but it seems to make life more interesting if we do.

Valerie Williams, 15 year old pupil, Chiltern Edge School,
Sonning Common, Oxfordshire (1969).

IN THE UPPER FORMS of the Secondary school, Family History can be pursued in really satisfying depth. The different directions in which projects can be developed in order to suit particular needs are well illustrated by the three following reports, the first from a history specialist particularly interested in developing his pupils' historical understanding, the second from a teacher primarily concerned with the social education of non-academic school leavers, and the third from a sixth-form student going on to university. An important point that emerges from the first two accounts is the value of sustaining an experiment over a number of years, modifying its structure and content in the light of experience.

A HISTORICAL ENQUIRY
with 3rd year Grammar school boys (Aged 13-14)
Colin Edwards, History Master, Stoneham School, Reading

Colin Edwards evolved a brand of Family History suited to the needs of Grammar School pupils, and his work, like that of the Maiden Erlegh team, was featured in the B.B.C. television programme, *Family History*.

Report

The First Experiment, 1968-69
In the first year, the project included the compiling of a family tree and the writing of a long essay on a topic associated with the family. For example, one boy became interested in the development of railways by discovering that his family had been concerned with early railways in Derbyshire for several generations. However, this 'open ended' approach, while giving the more able boys an excellent chance to illustrate their capabilities, placed too much responsibility upon the shoulders of the less able, who found it difficult to plan their material in order to fill the large amount of time left for private study. It appeared that the project needed to be more highly structured in order to assist pupils to work in depth.

The Second Experiment, 1969-70
The work was planned in much greater detail. After family trees and retrographs had been compiled, major political events such as the General Strike, or the Second World War were entered vertically on the retrographs. This associated the individual families more specifically with historical events over the last 100 years. Several mini-patches were then undertaken, working backwards from the present: 'Life in the Second World War', 'Life in the Depression' and 'The General Strike'. This approach seemed to achieve more success in terms of output than the previous year, and many interesting discoveries were made, particularly with reference to the Depression. It appeared that families were anxious to disguise poverty occasioned by unemployment and that shoes were a very important symbol. In one family the parents preferred to send their son to school wearing the mother's shoes rather than to admit to his having no shoes at all. The difficulty now arose, however, as to how to utilise the information from all the families. This was particularly important for those pupils who had not gained sufficient co-operation from their parents and whose accounts were consequently limited. At that time, the only solution appeared to be class discussion, and this tended to lead away from the family into a more general discussion of the topic. While the subject-matter was both useful and enjoyable, it seemed that we had, nevertheless, rather lost the idea of Family History. Although the boys' motivation was good and some excellent work was produced, in attempting to rectify the mistakes of the previous year I had undertaken 20th-century patch studies, copiously illustrated by information from the individual family histories. This was viable both educationally and historically, but it was not Family History. What was needed was a scheme which blended the best of the two extremes that had been attempted.

The Third Experiment, 1970-71
The introduction of the Family Tree and retrograph was followed by a series of questionnaires asking for information about such topics as upbringing, marriage-age, occupations and the homes of parents and grandparents (referred to as Generations 2 and 3). Although the sample was restricted in this instance to 72 boys, 144 parents and a possible 288 grandparents, there is no reason why a larger sample could not be obtained, or why further fields of questioning could not be explored. Using the statistics we had gained, and which had been individually compiled by the pupils, a picture of family life and home conditions was built up. Accounts were then written by pupils on these topics, where possible using additional information from their own families. The pooling of statistics enabled all pupils to contribute a great deal. The approach generated considerable interest and some useful work. The

Plates 82 and 83. Family History in progress, Stoneham School, Reading

statistics led to other questions. For example 'Why do occupations appear to have changed so much over the last 70-80 years?' or 'Why has the marriage age for women dropped during the last 70 years?'. The answers lay in a more detailed study of the problems, and discussion of the latter led on to a study of the growth of women's rights. This was more keenly undertaken as necessary to explain a question that had arisen out of the personal research of the pupils involved. The blend that was needed appears to have been made and this Family History project was very successful.

A SOCIAL STUDY

with 5th year Secondary Modern C.S.E. pupils (Aged 16), and 4th year Comprehensive school leavers (Aged 14-15).

Eddie McCall, History Master, Wick Hill County Secondary School, Bracknell New Town, merged in Garth Hill, a new comprehensive school with nearly 2,000 pupils.

Eddie McCall works in one of the largest comprehensive schools in the country. The fact that it is in a New Town makes it a relatively unfavourable school for Family History work. Many of the pupils' parents are young, in new houses with little room for lumber. When older parents move to New Towns they often destroy their accumulated family 'debris'. Moreover, few of Mr. McCall's pupils had grandparents living in the area. Yet he shows that despite all such disadvantages, a Family History scheme can be both profitable and rewarding, and his work is of particular interest in view of the raising of the school leaving age.

Report

The First Experiment, 1968-69: 5th year C.S.E. Class

It was originally planned to run two parallel Family History projects with the 5th year. My colleague sent duplicated letters to parents of his group, explaining the purpose of the project and inviting their co-operation. Out of 15 letters, about 12 met with point-blank refusals, some expressing concern that the children were being encouraged to pry. Forewarned, but undaunted by this experience, I decided not to approach parents immediately but to see what their reaction would be once the project was, in fact, under way. Although several parents proved unco-operative, the majority were helpful and none expressed outright hostility. Undoubtedly, it is a major tactical error to invite parental co-operation at the start.

Since the project was being undertaken with older pupils and time was limited, the *Who Am I?* stage was omitted, and the children set to work collecting data on their family backgrounds. This was a mistake. They needed to be familiarised with the idea that history has not just happened in the past to other people, but involves everybody.

Living in a New Town, most of the children had left their relatives in London or elsewhere. Not only did this mean that pupils had access to very few family photographs and documents, but most of their families were cut off from their relatives, both physically and psychologically. It would appear that in the case of these children, at any rate, the family was virtually non-existant — both the children and their parents seemed rootless. Teaching in a New Town, it is interesting to see how neighbours and friends seem to become a substitute extended family, and are frequently given the title of 'Aunt' or 'Uncle'. At the time, I was teaching sociology and economics and was extensively involved in youth work, and was particularly interested in the social aspects of a Family History scheme.

After their initial enquiries from parents, the pupils wrote letters to their relatives requesting information — in all the 15 pupils wrote 92 letters between them. The quality of the replies varied. Some gave simple yes/no answers; others were tremendously detailed. For this reason, a standard questionnaire was designed for further letters. A major difficulty was the delay between sending the letters and receiving the replies. We had only just under three months for the whole project, and collecting basic data took the best part of three weeks. The project almost came to a standstill towards the end of that period. The time was used to study changes in wages, prices and conditions of work and apprenticeship over the last generation, a subject which appeared to interest the children more than the Second World War. In collecting data on wages, it was interesting to see how some fathers sent in a comprehensive list up to the present, whereas understandably, others gave a very limited list, in one case ending in 1950. Although the more enthusiastic children used this period profitably, those who were only mildly interested became discontented. This was the low point of the project, and in later years such a limbo period was avoided by using this time for building up a card-index of information.

Surprisingly, many children were not aware even of the existence of relatives as close as parents' brothers and sisters. Some parents were unenthusiastic about renewing links. One boy, with a particularly bad home background, had tried unsuccessfully to trace his paternal grandfather. All his father could tell him was that his Grandad had been put into an old people's home in London. He could not even say which. After some searching in directories we located a possible home, and the boy sent off his letter. No reply was received for quite a long time. Eventually, the letter was returned with a covering note from another London home. The old man had been transferred from one home to another and had finally died only a few weeks before the letter had arrived. The Home had no knowledge of the whereabouts of any relatives. This was very sad, for perhaps this link with his grandfather may have helped the boy to adjust to life.

At the end of this first attempt, it was difficult to assess what the children or I had got out of the Family History Experience. Some of the children had taken a real interest in their family and its background. These would no doubt go on to find out more relatives and contact them. Others, after a disappointing start when they were unable to locate relatives, lost interest and saw the project as irrelevant to them. A few parents refused to give any information at all about their relatives.

The Second Experiment, 1969-70: Group of 15 14-15 year old school leavers

This was a first attempt to introduce the topic to 4th year leavers as part of their Social Studies course. The group was of mixed ability; some were relatively able but keen to leave school at the earliest opportunity; others were of very limited ability. Because the time allocated was still only two periods a week for one term, although a *Who Am I?* stage was included this time, it was limited to an introductory couple of lessons, perhaps again a mistake. After the *Who Am I?* introduction, the children set about collecting information about parents, and then, using the same questionnaire, sent out letters to relatives. A considerable display was made of photographs, medals, books etc. Although initial attitudes to the project varied, on the whole the first few weeks were really productive.

Statistical work was undertaken, and various tables were constructed showing family size and the way in which the number of children had declined. It was interesting to see how the same families tended to be larger in every generation. We also started a locational index, a series of maps showing where the pupil was born, and then the birthplaces of his parents and grandparents.

One boy was born on board a ship going to Malta, and this brought out other stories of unlikely birthplaces. When all the maps were put together, although most families came from London, all parts of England, Ireland Scotland and Wales were represented and one or two European countries. To further expand the material, we began a card-index. The children selected a topic from a list devised by the group and then proceeded to collect relevant information. One boy chose *wages* and collected sample wage rates for a variety of jobs. Others chose *food prices, furniture prices* etc. This proved to be less exciting than the locational index. Some children were able to make a large number of cards containing a wealth of information, whilst others could not or would not produce any. Those who made a large number seemed reluctant to share their information with those who had little to contribute — a competitive attitude which perhaps reflects more unfavourably on teachers and parents than on the children.

Although the second year of the project saw some innovations, basically the format was the same as the previous year. The greatest difficulty was that the project lasted for only a term, and so we could not take advantage of the contacts made by many families at Christmas time. However, some social contacts were undoubtedly strengthened and new ones made. One boy was able to trace his ancestry back to Austria, and made contact with a branch of the family there. He kept up some correspondence and was talking about going to Austria for a holiday to meet his relatives. Another boy became interested in the First World War. He found out that his grandfather (whom he very rarely saw) was a mine of war stories, and so started visiting him every week. Such contact with old people was, I think, one of the most valuable aspects of the project. Most old people do have interesting stories to tell, but all too often they are not approached.

The Third Experiment, 1970-71: Group of 22 school leavers — all boys

The project was again undertaken with fourth year leavers but this time it was carried out in conjunction with the English specialist, he and I having four periods a week each. So although it still only lasted a term, four times as much time was spent on it. The emphasis of the whole project was on society and the community, one of us approaching it through the family and the other through the locality.

The *Who Am I?* part of the project was slightly extended, but even so, the time we could afford to spend on this was limited. However this year it did succeed in introducing the pupils to the idea of the individual and the family as part of history.

While I was undertaking *Who Am I?*, my colleague was doing a parallel *Where Am I?* This involved mapping the district, photographing new developments in the Town Centre, and acquiring details of factories in the area. The boys also produced a map showing the location of their house, with a sketch of each.

One difficulty of having more than one teacher involved in the topic is lack of communication, and it proved vital that we knew what each of us was doing. It was too easy just to continue as if the local and family aspects of the project were quite separate.

After *Who Am I?*, the group set about collecting information about relatives, using the 1968 questionnaire. To try and forestall the 'limbo' period, I introduced the card-index and locational index very early in the term. This meant that the work being done by the group was varied, and most of the time the boys were working on different topics.

The old problem of those who lost interest again arose. The worst case was that of a boy whose parents refused to co-operate, and after trying to jog along by himself, he gave up completely. I thought of giving him the job of keeping the card-index, but this idea was a non-starter as once again most of the group jealously guarded their cards, and refused to put them in the card-box with a sliding lid specially made for the purpose by one of the boys in woodwork, which remained sadly unused. (No answer has yet been found to combat this excess of individualism). I decided to assign him to work with another boy. However, they did not get on with each other. In the end I put him with another boy who would accept him. They worked together for only a few lessons before they had to be separated. The problem was finally resolved by giving the boy a project of his own unconnected with Family History.

Despite the fact that the card-index never became really a group one, the cards did prove their worth on a number of occasions. Twins in the class had a relative who was an undertaker, and they were able to bring details of burial costs which entertained the rest of the class for some time.

We also had quite a substantial collection of photographs and birth, marriage and death certificates, all of which helped to fill out the data on the family trees. One difficulty here was that parents who supplied them were naturally unwilling to let them out of their sight for more than a few days. In some cases details were copied down and the certificates returned. This does however, prevent an effective display.

On the whole, apart from the exceptions already mentioned, the class took to the project quite well. The quantity and quality of work varied considerably. Some were able to produce quite detailed accounts of their families' progress, mapping their moves, and citing examples of relatives who were involved in the General Strike or the two World Wars.

The Personal Topic

Towards the end of the term, some of the group were already branching out to pursue topics in greater detail. One boy whose father had been in the Air Force during the last War completed a magnificent project on 'Aircraft of World War II'. Another, where the family had always been interested in building, produced a massive project on modern building materials contrasting them with traditional methods. He began by comparing his home in Bracknell with his house in London and from here became more involved in the technical side of house building and design.

Conclusion

Of the three experiments, perhaps the 1970-71 project was the most successful, though it was also the most difficult to organise.

Not only does the teacher need thoroughly to familiarise himself with the general social and economic background of the periods and social classes covered by the majority of the family histories, but he must give considerable time and thought to resourcing the project. I found that the most interested were continually running out of work. They would complete an assignment at home, and start a further assignment when they returned to school.

All three projects were based mainly on personal memories, given orally or by letter. We did not have time to consult many documentary sources, apart from those found in the home. This meant that all the family trees were short: many included great-grandparents, but few went back much further. With a more flexible timetable, it would have been interesting to go further back, using Somerset House and other record repositories. However, four generations proved adequate for a successful project, as my aims were sociological rather than genealogical.

A SIXTH-FORM ASSIGNMENT
John Higgs, pupil, Stoneham School, Reading, 1968-70

The relatively sophisticated research techniques employed by John Higgs add weight to the contention that 'A' level studies should not necessarily be wholly pre-occupied by studying history from secondary sources. Admittedly not all sixth formers would have John's inclination or capacity to devote themselves so vigorously to a difficult task, nor would they all be as fortunate as he was in having ancestors within 30 miles of their present home. Nevertheless, there are other adult varieties of Family History than the genealogically based approach followed by John. We hope to deal with these in future Branching Programme books, *The Apprentice Historian* and *Crossing the Frontiers*. (See pp. 49-50.)

Report
Genealogical Stage
The foundation for the genealogical stage of the project was laid by my paternal grandparents who were able to remember many significant dates of births, marriages and deaths of my grand-father's mother and father, aunts and uncles. I was able to trace the marriage certificate of my great-grandparents at the local registry office, thus by-passing an initial visit to Somerset House. I followed the lead of this certificate to Newbury and Speen where I searched the parish records and found a mass of Higgs entries which were very difficult to sort out, as several different families of this name had originated from the town. Fortunately, I discovered a

book containing genealogical tables of several Higgs families, including those at Newbury. With the aid of this and my own notes, I was able to trace back another three generations. My research led me back to the parish registers of Reading and Caversham, where I found another hundred years of Higgs entries. I succeeded in sorting out those which were relevant, and by using them in conjunction with wills at the Bodleian Library, I was able to take my pedigree back a further two generations to c.1700.

Biographical Stage

Unable to trace my ancestry back any further, I began to broaden my interests, searching records like churchwarden's accounts, tithe maps, apprentice lists, trade directories, census returns and local newspapers. I also made detailed searches at Somerset House, obtaining numerous birth, marriage and death certificates and post-1858 wills. This work greatly increased my interest in the subject, as I usually found some reference to one of my ancestors. I have now developed a filing system for my records and am making detailed studies of my ancestors' occupations, their houses and the churches they used.

The Value of a Sixth Form Family History Project

The encouragement of Family History in sixth forms would seem to be an ideal way of introducing the student to work with documents and on his own. My studies gave me an insight into the use of· documents in historical research, and I am now able to read 17th and 18th century manuscripts fairly easily, which I hope will be of use to me in my further education. Through reading local newspapers, I found that this contemporary view of historical events helped to stimulate my interest in the political history course which I was following, and would have been equally useful in social and economic history.

Problems

Despite its great advantages as a sixth-form assignment, this form of personal research has its drawbacks. The cost may be prohibitive, for both travel and copying can, and often do, prove expensive. Furthermore, relevant documents may have been lost or destroyed or may have never existed.

I believe that sixth-form History or General Studies teachers should have a sound knowledge of sources for both family history and local history and should give active support and encouragement to projects based on them. A course of lessons on the use of such documents would give the student a sounder basis of knowledge, so that he can choose for himself whether he wishes to work on a Family History or Local History project. In either case the student would be given some experience of how history is written, which should be an essential part of any sixth-form history course.

*   *   *   *

New approaches to history, as with other subjects, tend to find a place in the school curriculum a generation after they have attained academic respectability. In the first three decades of the 20th century, the Hammonds, the Coles, Postgate and Tawney made the history of the common man a fit subject for study by scholars, and by the late 1930s Social History was being widely taught in schools. The cult of the common man in its turn led to the forging by Hoskins, Finberg, Emmison, Tate and others of a new type of Local History rooted in, but radically different from its antiquarian ancestor. Today, the idea of investigating how the common man lived and worked in one's own area is having a noticeable impact on the schools. Can one dare to hope that with Family History it will be the teachers who will show the historians the validity of the approach?

Index

PHASE I

WHO AM I?

Generation 1 (c.1960-The Future)

Unit 1 : My Family
Unit 2 : My Life
Unit 3 : A Changing World
Unit 4 : The Future
Unit 5 : Evaluation

PHASE 2

INVOLVING THE PARENTS

Generation 2 (c.1930-date)

Unit 6 : Parents' Childhoods
Unit 7 : World War II: The
          Home Front
Unit 8 : Post-War Britain
Unit 9 : My Family Tree
Unit 10 : Evaluation

RESOURCES

PRIMARY SOURCES

Oral Evidence
Family Documents
Photographs
Newspapers

Classroom Museum
School Records
Maps
Genealogical Sources